THE CUBAN INVASION

THE CUBAN INVASION

The Chronicle of a Disaster

by KARL E. MEYER *and* TAD SZULC

FREDERICK A. PRAEGER
Publisher • New York

BOOKS THAT MATTER

Published in the United States of America in 1962 by
Frederick A. Praeger, Inc., Publisher
64 University Place, New York 3, N.Y.

Library of Congress Catalog Card Number: 62-15262

Published simultaneously in paperback by Ballantine Books, Inc.

Manufactured in the United States of America

CONTENTS

It is the tragedy of a world where man must walk by sight that the discovery of the reconciling formula is always left to future generations, in which passion has cooled into curiosity, and the agonies of peoples have become the exercise in the schools. The devil who builds bridges does not span such chasms till much that is precious to mankind has vanished down them forever.

—R. H. TAWNEY

PROLOGUE

A few minutes before three o'clock on the morning of Monday, April 17, 1961, a landing craft filled with silent men in jungle camouflage uniforms nosed into the sand of Playa Girón; just east of the entrance to the Bay of Pigs on the swampy coast of southern Cuba. About thirty minutes later, other landing craft touched land at Playa Larga, a tree-bordered beach at the apex of the Bay. Within minutes, the dry crackling of M-1 rifles and the staccato fire of Thompson submachine guns echoed along the dark beaches, punctuated now and then by the thud of bazooka rockets hitting the high ground.

The air waves of the Caribbean came alive with weird, exciting words about the rising red moon and the running fish. At hidden strips in Nicaragua and Guatemala, B-26 bombers and C-54 transport planes revved up their engines, ready to take off with their load of bombs and paratroopers. And when daylight broke over the Cuban shores, a full-scale miniature invasion, materializing from phantom bases, was underway.

For the next 72 hectic, incredible hours, Operation Pluto —the attack on Fidel Castro's fortress by a band of brave but totally unprepared Cuban exiles—ran its inexorable course toward defeat. When it was over, the incident on the Bay of Pigs earned its place in the annals of modern history as one of the great fiascos in military leadership, intelligence gathering, and psychological preparation and execution.

Invasions had failed before, but seldom had a great power like the United States allowed itself to be caught in so embarrassing a predicament as in the attack on Cuba, mounted, financed and executed by the Central Intelligence Agency. The military implications of the disaster were obvious: an operation bearing the stamp of approval of the Joint Chiefs of Staff of the world's most powerful nation was destroyed in less than three days by half-trained, part-time militia troops of a disorganized, revolutionary state led by a bearded guerrilla leader who had somehow taught his men to use with devastating effect the most modern Czech and Soviet weapons.

But the political repercussions were even more humiliating. As the invasion approached its tragic denouement, the United States buried itself deeper into the white lies, contradictions and deceptions stemming from its own confusion and uncertainty. There was the poignant spectacle of Adlai E. Stevenson, the respected Ambassador to the United Nations, telling the world forum that the planes that had bombed Castro's airfields—and missed their targets—were defecting Cuban aircraft, when it was painfully evident that they had come from the United States-built Guatemalan bases. There were the words of Secretary of State Dean Rusk declaring on the morning of the landing that it was a purely Cuban undertaking.

And, as perhaps the strangest counterpoint to the drama that was unfolding in the Cuban marshes, there was the stunned bewilderment of the Cuban Revolutionary Council —the men in whose name the invasion was being carried out—as they learned from a portable radio in a shack at the abandoned airfield of Opa-Locka in Florida where they were being held in friendly custody that their troops had gone ashore.

The backdrop was in accord with the rest of the phantasmagoric operation. A New York press agent was handing out war communiqués, drafted in the style of a great army's headquarters, that were telephoned to him by an exiled Cuban judge, who in turn was receiving them from the CIA. His assistants were signing up news correspondents for the trip to the beachhead that was to start any minute, but they never left the lobbies of Miami hotels. In a private house in Georgetown, ten minutes away from the White House, a small dinner celebration was underway—until the news from the elusive front, relayed by walkie-talkies from the bloody and swampy beach to a United States destroyer laying offshore, turned the party into a mournful wake.

No melodramatic and tragicomical touch was missing in the hours that Operation Pluto lived its short life as the strangest tragedy of errors in which the United States was ever involved.

When it was all over and only the tears, the anger and the recrimination were left, the great question arose of how such a debacle could have occurred.

How indeed did events move in the 27 months of the

Cuban revolution to a point where the United States resolved to stake its prestige on a thoughtless, madcap operation against an island republic that in its more than half century of nominal independence had been little more than an exotic appendage to the State of Florida?

CHAPTER ONE

➪ THE SEARCH FOR A DEVIL

The history of the Cuban revolution has an air of inevitability about it in the grand manner of classical tragedy, in which the myriad actors seem fated to perform their assigned roles although they know the drama is bound to end in calamity.

Finding the plot is no simple matter. Among Fidel Castro's incontrovertible gifts is the ability to cloud his course in confusion, like a squid emitting ink as it retreats to the deep. He performed a superb job on his own people, and as the melancholy events of April 17, 1961, testify, the meaning of his movement clearly mystified the Central Intelligence Agency. Hence it is a formidable task to unravel the knots that compose the web of Cuban-American relations 1959-1961.

Some threads lead nowhere, and belong to the fabric of deception that Dr. Castro, or some of his cohorts, wove carefully from the day the rebels set foot in the Sierra Maestra. Others constitute myths that ought to be pulled from the knot.

The first myth, favored by those who see all history as a murky conspiracy, is that the Cuban revolution was plotted in the Kremlin and subsequently abetted by shadowy subversives on the sixth floor of the State Department. But the record suggests that what happened in Cuba was as much a surprise to Moscow as to Washington—notwithstanding Dr. Castro's confession that he had long ago become a Marxist-Leninist. If any conspiracy existed, it was a conspiracy of circumstance that pitted a large, affluent nation led by complacent men who had forgotten the meaning of a revolution against a proud, small country led by gifted and intolerantly zealous men.

A second myth, propounded by Castro's well-wishers in

9

Latin America and the United States, is that drastic social changes in Cuba were impossible without scuttling democratic methods and provoking the implacable hostility of the United States. Retrospect suggests that Cuba could have pursued its revolutionary goals in a democratic fashion with at least the passive acquiescence of Washington—which was anxious to come to terms with a revolution it hardly understood—if the leaders in Havana had not been determined to confirm their darkest suspicions about Yankee imperialism by inviting the very retaliation they professed to dread. Doubtless the United States was clumsy, but there should not be excessive masochism about American ineptitude; for reasons of pure revolutionary dynamics—aside from communism—the Castro regime could not flourish without anti-Americanism.

All this leads to the final and special myth about the invasion itself. Some contend that the only thing wrong with the venture was that it was poorly done. If there had only been an air cover by United States planes, one argument runs, the invasion would have succeeded. It is our contention that the invasion was not only wrongly executed but wrongly conceived.

It was based on a grievous misreading of the Cuban revolution and an ignorance of the internal forces at work on the island. It put the United States in the distressing position of breaking the same treaties that Dr. Castro had been exhorted to respect, and it raised grave questions about compromising the institutions on which a free society rests. It did all this without shedding needed light on the very real dilemma of how to counteract the "wars of national liberation" that Mr. Khrushchev has vowed to support. This dilemma did not end with the April invasion and it may be posed again as internal discontent on Dr. Castro's captive island rises once more.

These are some of the myths. In trying to unsnarl the knot, a more promising lead lies in the thread of inevitability that runs through the entire unhappy history. From the beginning, the specter of impending tragedy was apparent; it was bound to materialize when impatient and frustrated men felt impelled to turn a sword on the Gordian knot.

II

The seed of tragedy began to germinate in Havana almost from the day that Fidel Castro plummeted into the

10

capital after his triumphant march across the island in January 1959 proclaiming that the defeat of the Batista dictatorship marked the beginning, and not the end, of Cuba's great revolution. In a deeper sense, to be sure, the seed had been planted when the United States ejected the Spaniards from Cuba at the turn of the century and then allowed the island to become a nominally sovereign republic, politically controlled from Washington and economically directed from New York's banks and big sugar houses.

For 57 years, since her independence was established in 1902, Cuba had functioned for all practical purposes as a dependent territory of the United States. Her political life, a grotesque chain of dictatorships and venal administration interrupted by short-lived attempts at revolutionary democracy, was manipulated by the State Department and the American Embassy in Havana. Huge tracts of her sugar land were owned by United States companies and, as Castro remarked in his famous speech in 1953 addressed to a Batista tribunal, the land owned by two sugar companies linked the northern and southern coasts of Oriente Province. Such industry as existed in Cuba was made up of subsidiaries of mainland corporations; the hotels and casinos were owned by American syndicates, often deeply infiltrated by gamblers and gangsters.

The relationship was scarcely healthy, and it was not surprising that Cuba's entire history was punctuated by fierce tides of anti-American sentiment. Still, it is important to note that this anti-American animus did not extend to the masses of Cubans, even in the subsequent hate-infected days when the Castro government had selected the United States for its chief target of invective and derision.

Gay, emotional and mercurial, the Cubans had by and large developed a comfortable rapport with Americans. In it, tolerance of American ways was mixed with some envy and a tendency toward imitation of the mainland mannerisms.

As a result, Havana—the country's showplace—turned into a lovely but weird caricature of a stateside pleasure town. Set against the natural beauty of the Caribbean and with its charming old Spanish streets and castles, the capital acquired the worst characteristics of Floridian, Californian and Nevadian garishness. Multicolor neon signs flickered at night, inviting the tourists to partake of pleasures in the small bars named "Joe's" or "Harry's," where sensuous fun girls were part of the atmosphere of rumbas and cha-cha-chas. Eight casinos, in which Batista and his friends participated

11

financially in varying degrees, catered to the American tourists and Cuban millionaires whose fortunes stemmed from sugar land and generous graft. In the suburbs, the elegant homes of American permanent residents and members of the Cuban ruling class were reminiscent of the best of the Gold Coast of Florida.

It was colonial life at its feudal, opulent and amusing best. The mainland was just one hour away, and Cuba's aristocracy commuted to the stateside metropolises to do business, to rest, to shop and to plot revolutions against the "ins" of the day.

The tinsel façade was supported by the labor of *guajiros* on the sugar plantations and of the city workers, thus spreading to the whole smiling island the utter distortion that a corrupt colonial life can cause. It is true that Cuba's living standards, measured by the Latin American yardstick, were fairly high. But it is also true that life in Cuba, taken as a whole, presented the image of a country seen in the distorting mirror of an amusement park—or through the wrong end of a telescope set up in the United States. The country was like a composite of West Germany and Egypt, affluence and harsh feudal poverty side by side. This very discrepancy helps to explain the accumulated tension that exploded into violent revolution.

Rebellion first arose in Cuba among politically conscious students and young professionals. The revolution against the Machado dictatorship in 1933 was a movement against political oppression as well as against graft—and the exaggerated American influence. A new generation fought against the same excesses after Batista's second *coup d'état* in 1952. And Fidel Castro and his leftist friends saw in all these ills the inspiration of a Cuba purified by revolution.

Despite all this, the Cuban masses were passive enough to turn out in hundreds of thousands to cheer Batista, even though students died in futile attacks on the Presidential Palace and army barracks. The sentiment against the United States was strong among young reformers, who saw American influence as the root of evil, but in the nation at large there was none of that sullen anti-Americanism that is found elsewhere in the world.

III

Yet, as Castro stepped upon the Cuban stage, there existed the tremendous potential of Cuban resentment against the United States government, a latent hostility that was aggravated during the two years of the rebellion against Batista by the Eisenhower Administration's frank attitude of sympathy for the entrenched dictatorship. The bearded fighters of the Sierra Maestra took as their theme the charge that American-made bombs sold to Batista and dropped by Batista fliers trained by United States military missions had killed civilians in the cities as well as rebel soldiers.

Therefore, Castro faced an immediate fundamental decision. Should he allow this natural resentment to run its course by ignoring it—as was done in the South American countries where military dictatorships favored by Washington were overthrown? Or should he feed, exploit and build up popular passions by making anti-Americanism a basic theme of his regime? Either choice was possible from a political viewpoint in those first, joyous, exhilarating days of the Castro triumph. There was no popular clamor against the United States, and the "Maximum Leader" was under little pressure to turn his guns on the Americans. Adored as he was by millions of Cubans, Castro had no need to practise demagogic anti-Americanism in order to win greater support.

To some degree, the United States had learned a lesson from the antidictatorial revolutions of the preceding years. There was talk about a warm *abrazo* for democrats and a cool handshake for dictators, and the United States was fairly bursting with anxiety to show its friendship for this latest revolution. On January 8, when hardly a week had elapsed, Washington granted diplomatic recognition to the new regime and the State Department hurried to assure it of America's "sincere good will."

There was, then, some basis for a new relationship between Cuba and the United States. But from the beginning it seems evident that Castro was determined that it was not to be so; the kind of revolution he evidently had in mind required an enemy image, uniting Cubans under a patriotic banner of resistance to a predatory foreign foe. The pattern is familiar. Other great revolutions needed foreign enemies to consolidate power at home and maintain dynamism. The French revolutionary armies marched into Italy and Germany for reasons more powerful than the need to dispose of scheming *émigrés*. The Soviet Union invaded Poland in 1920 for reasons that went beyond her anxiety to protect herself from the White Russian forces that attacked her at Vladivostok on the Sea of Japan. Communist China has been displaying her revolutionary dynamism and aggressiveness along her entire southeastern perimeter—and even so

13

mild a new nation as India felt impelled to reach out for Goa.

Fidel Castro could not very well invade the United States; instead he chose it as his political target and soon engaged in invasion attempts against four Caribbean and Central American countries, a prelude to the subsequent and more sophisticated efforts to "export" his revolution. Here, the parallel is closer to Colonel Nasser of Egypt, and there is ample reason to think that Castro saw himself as a comparable rallying symbol for an entire region.

Even when he was in the mountains, Castro saw the importance of his rebellion, not in national, but in hemisphere terms. Isolated as he was, his thinking was never insular; he viewed his movement as marking a turning-point for Latin America because it would demonstrate that a popular revolt could win fighting "neither with the army nor without the army—but *against* the army, contrary to all previous Latin American experience," as he told one of the authors at the time. "Condemn me! It doesn't matter!" Fidel cried at his 1953 trial for leading an attack against a Batista army barrack, "History will absolve me!" This familiar shout of defiance suggests that from the outset Castro saw himself as the chosen instrument of history and welded the personal pronoun to the cause he led.

Castro could hardly have realized his vaulting ambition as a junior partner to Washington; the elevation of his name required that he speak for the hemisphere in the role of avenging adversary. And the world, too, would pay attention if a David so close to Goliath let loose with a sling.

Before long, Castro began to rationalize his policy by arguing that the capitalistic United States, so influenced by business lobbies, would never stand still and accept a social revolution in what had for nearly six decades been a private American preserve. But the argument runs aground when it is recalled that Castro launched his anti-Yankee campaign, subtly at first, and then more and more openly and blatantly, months before the Agrarian Reform law went into effect, providing the United States with a conceivable reason for wanting to destroy his revolution.

This campaign was insinuatingly begun on January 13 in a speech Castro delivered before the Havana Rotary Club, in which he pointedly reminded his audience that Cuba had always been governed by foreigners and that the United States had forced the notorious Platt Amendment on Cuba as a license to intervene if "we do not behave."

"Cuba," he went on to say, "was not free because when

14

a foreigner arrogates for himself the right of intervening in the affairs of a country, that country is not free."

All this was palpably true; the Platt Amendment, abrogated in 1934, permitted the United States to intervene in Cuba and was one of the less glorious pages in American relations with weaker Latin American neighbors. But the timing and context of Castro's speech was significant, coming as it did in the opening days of the revolution at the very moment when the United States was casting about for ways of embracing the Cuban revolution with belated tenderness.

On January 13, therefore, the first link was forged in the chain of events that was to culminate in the debacle at the Bay of Pigs.

Part of the explanation may perhaps be found in Castro's admission that he was a Marxist-Leninist—a euphemism for Communist—for some time in the past. If so, then his hostility to the United States was ideologically motivated and his policies, unrolling gradually, were an impressively adroit performance designed to introduce communism in Cuba under the guise of defending the revolution from the island's giant neighbor, using the theme that to be anticommunist is to be antirevolutionary. This would have made the course of events until 1961 wholly inevitable, because the United States was bound to react against the establishment of a Communist state closely allied to the Soviet bloc ninety miles from Key West.

An incident that suggested the direction the Cuban revolution was taking occurred in Havana during March 1959, and involved Costa Rica's former President, José "Pepe" Figueres, the man who had dispatched the first airplane load of weapons to Castro in the Sierra Maestra. On its face, it seemed at the time like one of those hot-headed, nationalistic outbursts for which the Cuban revolutionaries were making themselves famous. But the follow-up was highly significant.

Figueres had come to Havana and found himself in the midst of a speech-making affair with Castro. When his turn at the microphone came, Figueres said, in the context of a general discussion of the position of Latin America in the world, that in case of a war the hemisphere, and Cuba, should stand with the United States and the Western alliance. The microphone was yanked away by David Salvador, the president of the Cuban Labor Federation, who roared to the crowd that Cuba under no circumstances should join the Americans in a war. The startled Figueres looked up to

15

Castro, as if hoping for a denial, but the "Maximum Leader" averted his eyes and failed to intervene.

The incident was a slap in the face for Figueres—an act of rudeness aimed at a man who had been one of the principal early supporters of the war against Batista. Yet, it would have been overlooked if Castro had not ten days later chosen to launch a personal attack on Figueres, calling him a "false friend" and a misguided revolutionary.

With this attack, we can see in retrospect, Castro drew the line between his movement and the democratic revolutionary tradition in Latin America. Other revolutionary movements in the hemisphere had an element of anti-Americanism, but this was related to a general opposition to dictators. The enemy for other revolutionaries was the dictator; for Castro, it became the United States.

As Theodore Draper has pointed out, Castro promised one kind of revolution and delivered another. Perhaps the reason was that the Cuban revolution was bound up in the personality of its champion, whose need for self-dramatization required something exceptionally daring and provocative. In addition, Marxist stereotypes played their part in shaping Castro's attitude toward the capitalist power of the north. The point that is significant is that Castro disguised these tendencies and seemed to speak in the accents of the general democratic movement in the hemisphere when he first came out of the mountains.

Curiously, it took a long time and repeated attacks by Castro on the democratic revolutionary tradition before much of Latin America—and even the liberal sector in the United States—slowly accepted the fact that the Cuban revolution was taking a highly dubious direction in its surge forward. Venezuela's President Rómulo Betancourt was one of the first to lose his illusions about Castro. As early as August 1959, he told friends privately that Castro was emerging as an evil problem in Latin America. Colombia's President Alberto Lleras Camargo was equally perturbed and prescient.

Yet, many Latin American democrats resisted these conclusions even after Castro, sounding like an angry Adolf Hitler, denounced both Betancourt and Lleras in that gutter language of revolutionary propaganda that became so common over Cuban air waves.

Taken all together, the actions of Fidel Castro in the first months of the revolution, seen in perspective and as explained by the Premier himself in his confession that he had disguised the radicalism of his movement in its early

16

days, laid part of the foundation for the whole unavoidable process of deterioration of Cuban-American relations, leading to the drama of the April invasion and doubtless to new dramatic chapters.

Yet this is not the whole story. While Castro himself had laid to rest the argument energetically advanced by many of his early sympathizers that the United States through its fumbling pushed Cuba into communism, the fact does remain that Washington's inability to understand the mechanics of revolution and the subtlety of Castro's policies played right into his hands. The United States abetted Castro's capture of his people and contributed vastly to the tragic cycle of events.

IV

During the first year of the revolution, the Castro regime operated on two levels. The first level, the visible part of the revolutionary iceberg, was the program of social reform hectically and enthusiastically advanced by a regime that initially included moderates who saw no real conflict between what they were setting in motion and a friendly relationship with the United States.

The second level was the quiet but nonetheless efficient process of transferring the levers of real power to a small group of communists and their ebullient bearded allies. The very existence of the hidden level of operation was indignantly denied by Castro and his companions and skeptically regarded by liberal opinion in the United States. Castro frequently denied that he was a communist and even expressed concern that communists might take over his movement. His "26th of July Movement" printed millions of stickers in English and Spanish proclaiming that "We Are Humanists and Not Communists." The procommunists in Castro's entourage made the denials for obvious tactical reasons. His moderate supporters denied it because they believed it or wanted to believe it. Years of extravagant and patently spurious charges of "communism" by Batista propagandists gave a ring of plausibility to the assertion that to every right-wing military dictator all foes are automatically "communist." Castro benefited by the scattershot defamation tactics of the Batista clique—whose members now, ironically, claim that they were "right" on asserting that only communists opposed Fulgencio Batista.

The fall of the moderates came late in November 1959, as the denouement of a power struggle that began in July,

17

when Castro dismissed President Manuel Urrutia Lleó and replaced him with Osvaldo Dorticós Torrado, an unknown provincial lawyer who, as it turned out later, was one of the most skillful members of the Cuban communist apparatus.

It is a moot point whether the moderates ever had a chance of carrying the day and keeping an obviously hesitant Fidel Castro under a modicum of their influence. Recalling those days in a speech in December 1961, Castro remarked that it was "convenient" at the time to have "conservatives" in his government. But it can be argued that these men—who, in fact, were far from being "conservative" in the accepted sense of the word—could have been more than just a convenience for Castro, if they had been given a chance.

And, as we shall see, there is a great body of evidence to suggest that private and public attitudes of the United States deprived them of this chance, undercut their position and virtually handed the victory to the extremists.

This, too, seemed inevitable, because the United States government and much American public opinion, including segments of the press, had not fully perceived the depth of the Cuban revolution. They insisted on treating it in their mind and through their actions, as just another Latin American political convulsion, although Castro almost every night was telling his own nation and the United States that this was a different revolution from anything yet seen in the Western Hemisphere. "We are," he said, "a small country making a big revolution."

Though the official pronouncements from Washington played intellectual lip service to the social aspects of the Cuban revolution, Cubans—radicals and moderates alike— were convinced that the United States simply had not understood what was happening under its nose despite its big embassy, its extensive intelligence network and its immense press so fascinated by Cuban events.

Premier Castro had convinced himself from the very beginning that the United States understood just enough of his revolution to be determined to smash it. This belief fitted perfectly into his early decision to portray Cuba as a victim of American imperialism and to use this impression as a lever to mobilize Cuban sentiment against the United States and then to carry his country to the extreme left. The United States obliged him fervently and blindly at a time when the communists were still far from complete control and the moderates still had at least a fighting chance.

The first point about the Cuban revolution in its early

stages—and the point that the United States seemed to have missed altogether—was that it was a transfiguring emotional experience. It was the release of pent-up feelings of frustration, it was an overwhelming welling up of pride, it was a dizzying sense of participation in building a new nation and a new epoch. It was zeal, dedication, excitement. And it was a raw-nerve feeling of sensitivity about the whole undertaking. "What do you think of *our* revolution?" was the first question that met American visitors.

The American response, more often than not, was dry, legalistic and phlegmatic. To be sure, much good will existed in the first weeks and even months of the revolution. Six United States companies in Havana advanced to the Castro regime $1,500,000 in future taxes to help the "Maximum Leader" stabilize the stricken economy. American managers of sugar mills and plantations who had seen their workers grow from childhood and then helped them hide from the Batista forces, were still seen as friends instead of the imperialist monsters of subsequent times.

But, as will be recounted in the next chapter, this good will was largely wiped away by the shocked and sanctimonious American reaction to the wave of mass executions of "war criminals" that Cubans regarded as substantially just, even though scarcely measuring up to the procedural standards of Anglo-Saxon law.

V

Then there was the problem of the exiles. On January 19, Castro appealed to the United States to "return war criminals and the money they stole," in reference to the hundreds of Batista officials who had fled to Florida with suitcases full of pesos. The United States ignored the appeal. This suited Castro and played into the hands of those who were engaged in making the United States appear as the hypocritical enemy of the beloved revolution.

Presumably, the United States could not deport the Batista refugees to Cuba to face certain death—and Castro assuredly knew this. But the United States could and should have prevented the exiles from plotting against the revolutionary regime, smuggling weapons into Cuba and sending light planes to throw incendiary bombs on the sugar fields.

On March 7, Castro charged that the enemies of the revolution were buying up arms in Miami, and on March 24 he warned that "reactionary Americans" were planning an invasion. Whether or not his charges were justified, the

19

fact is that a Batista organization known as the "White Rose" began functioning in Miami. Such activities could hardly have served the best interests of the United States and it is astonishing that American authorities were unable or unwilling to prevent them. This policy, or lack of a policy, made little sense at a moment when Philip W. Bonsal, the new United States Ambassador chosen for his reputation as a liberal, was telling Cubans in Havana of Washington's sympathy for the revolution.

A charitable explanation is that one arm of the United States Government did not know what the other arm was doing, a bureaucratic phenomenon that was repeated with more fateful results on April 17, 1961. But it was incomprehensible to the Cubans; Castro and his companions exultantly pointed to this evidence of United States duplicity.

On July 1, Major Pedro Luis Díaz Lanz, chief of the Cuban air force, turned up in Florida after he had fled the island by boat some days before. Ten days later he was delivered by the Immigration and Naturalization Service, a division of the Justice Department, to the Senate Internal Security Subcommittee, where he testified that communists were taking over Cuba.

The news of his appearance shocked Cubans in Havana as well as the State Department and Central Intelligence Agency. Although some of Major Díaz Lanz's accusations turned out to be true, the circumstances of his appearance played right into Castro's hand. The Premier charged immediately that the United States had intervened in Cuban affairs and he would not accept the explanation that the Executive Branch had nothing to do with it. The occasion provoked Castro's first violently anti-American speech.

The entire Díaz Lanz affair dealt a devastating blow to the moderates in the revolutionary regime who opposed the now visible communist infiltration and advocated closer ties with the United States. As one former moderate-minded minister put it, "This shut us up." Thus the United States became actively engaged in the suicidal process of undercutting its friends within the Cuban government.

An immediate result of the incident was the removal of President Urrutia by Castro in a wild speech before a battery of television cameras. Urrutia's sin had been to couple his denunciation of Díaz Lanz as a traitor with an attack on communism, and his punishment at Castro's hands was an extraordinary feat of character assassination.

By then, the over-all American reaction to the social revolution had already begun to weaken the moderates and

20

strengthen the extremists by handing the latter faction the argument that nothing favorable could be expected from the United States.

The land-reform law had been promulgated in May. The United States reaction was to express the hope that prompt and effective compensation would be paid to the American owners of expropriated land. It was, to be sure, the proper juridical attitude, but it failed to take account of the psychological transformation of Cuba.

Cuba is basically an agricultural country. The notion of distributing lands to the peasants and in theory making them smallholders had enormous appeal and the program rapidly became the most popular measure of the revolutionary regime. It should not have come as a surprise to the United States because Castro had mentioned agrarian reform at length in his 1953 defense speech—his famous "History Will Absolve Me" exhortation—and talked about it interminably in the Sierra Maestra.* After he took office in Havana, he repeatedly spoke of the need for land reform. Yet Washington reacted as if the agrarian reform had dropped from the sky, and it responded with a prissy legalism that chilled its best friends in Havana.

This inability to understand the revolution remained the counterpoint to the entire history of Washington's relations with Castro's Cuba. Cubans are warm and emotional; the land reform had caught their imagination. Hotel elevators, operators greeted callers with the slogan, "The Land Reform Is Moving," and Carlos Puebla, the popular composer and singer made up a song about it that thousands sang and whistled.

But to Washington, the reform was a question of the payment of compensation, although it was perfectly clear that Cuba was in no position to do more than promise twenty-year land bonds. That Castro never bothered even to print the bonds is beside the point; the United States did not have to give him the pretext for ridiculing its response to the law.

Throughout, the Eisenhower Administration seemed to

---

*Specifically, in that speech Castro described the second revolutionary law as granting the untransferable title of property "to all the tenants [colonos], subtenants, leasees . . . who occupied lots of five or less caballerias [a cab is 33 acres], with the state indemnifying its former owners on the basis of the rent they would have derived from the land in a ten-year average." The fourth revolutionary law would have given a share of sugar revenues to all tenants.

21

concentrate on the material impact of the revolution, overlooking the immensely important emotional ingredients that came with the pride in regained sovereignty and the elimination of graft and boodle.

As it was, Castro was firmly convinced by mid-July 1959 that history was moving his way and that his revolution had found the enemy image that it needed. One of the authors sat up all night with Castro listening to him expound his theory that the United States simply *had* to fight his revolution, then rationalize his decision to cancel the promised elections. Faced with such a formidable adversary, he explained, the revolution could not afford the luxury of the democratic process. As we talked in the kitchen of a Havana hotel, an aide handed Castro a news-agency dispatch quoting Admiral Arleigh Burke, then Chief of Naval Operations, as saying that communists are "using" the Premier.

Castro read it, then remarked with visible satisfaction, "You see? They're against us. Every day something new."

VI

Indeed, the accusations of communism aimed at the revolution with growing frequency from the United States handed Castro a powerful weapon for equating anticommunism with counterrevolution. He developed this theme skillfully in convincing the Cubans that the United States was using the "ghost" of anticommunism to derail the revolution. Cubans were sufficiently enamored of the revolution to accept this simple formula, and the way was open for the liquidation of the moderates and the ultimate victory of the communists.

Here again we encounter the thread of inevitability. If on the one hand the United States government and public opinion could not ignore the emerging importance of communism in Cuba, every warning against communism tended to strengthen this very penetration by the procommunist left. There was no way the United States could win.

Still, it can be argued that if the United States had not helped Castro by putting America in the position of seeming an enemy of the revolution, then the moderates could have tempered the swing to extremism and Castro would have had a far harder time in putting the devil's horns on the United States.

From the beginning, Castro's own relationship to the communists was ambiguous, despite his recent avowal of Marxist-Leninist sympathies. After the 1953 attack on the Army barracks in Santiago, the Communist Party in Cuba dismissed him as an "ordinary putschist." When the Castro underground in Havana called a general strike in April 1958, the communists refused to participate. Having taken part in the Batista cabinet in 1940, they were still supporting the dictator. It was not until late in 1958 that Carlos Rafael Rodríguez, the theorist of the Cuban Party, went up to the Sierra Maestra to confer with Castro. The formal pact between Castro and the communists for their participation in the anti-Batista movement was signed days before the victory of the revolution. In his speech in December 1961, Castro took the occasion to remark that he wished that the revolution could have been made with the communists from the beginning, "as they did in Russia."

It is worth recalling that when Castro entered the mountains in December 1956, Nikita Khrushchev was still a relatively new figure on the world stage and that the bloody age of Stalin still dominated the popular impression of Russia. The Khrushchev policy of aiding wars of "national liberation" was germinating, and the memory of the Hungarian uprising was fresh. Equally important, the United States at that time cast a more pervasive shadow in Latin America. By the time Castro emerged from the mountains, the world had taken a different shape, presenting new possibilities for defying the Yankee giant with the benevolent help of Moscow.

At the same time Castro was surrounded in the Sierra by a group of communist sympathizers, notably Major Ernesto "Ché" Guevara. Fidel's brother Raúl commanded a nucleus of communist officers on his "Second Front" in Sierra Cristal. There were reports that Raúl had court-martialed several officers for expressing anticommunist views while others were forced to leave the rebel army. Among those purged was Captain Jorge Sotús, the first officer to be commissioned in the mountains from outside Fidel's original invasion force.

William Morgan, the American volunteer who commanded anti-Batista forces in the Sierra Escambray and who was later executed by Castro, told one of the authors that when Major Guevara led his rebel column from the Sierra Maestra across Camagüey and Las Villas provinces, he made a practice of leaving communist officers in every town and village along the way. Morgan and Guevara met in Las Villas, and a battle between them was narrowly averted when the American commander tried to disarm the Argentine.

Until July 1959, direct communist participation in the

23

revolutionary regime was limited. Castro said later that this was deliberate and unavoidable. But the fact remains that during this period the moderates and anticommunists held considerable power.

At first, Major Guevara was restricted to the command of La Cabaña Fortress in Havana; then he was sent on a trip to neutralist nations. The only important extremists in high position were Raúl Castro as commander of the armed forces, Armando Hart, Minister of Education, Major Juan Almeida, the army commander, and Captain Antonio Núñez Jiménez, head of the National Institute of Agrarian Reform.

But, imperceptibly at first, the communists were making progress. Although Castro banned all political parties, the Socialist Popular Party (communist) was allowed to function and to publish its newspaper, *Hoy*. When asked about this inconsistent exception by one of the authors, Castro shrugged and said, "Well, they are not important." Then he added quickly, "But they are in favor of the revolution and you Americans are against it."

An important gain made by the communists during this period was their capture of the Army's G-2 branch, the secret service, which laid the groundwork for their subsequent success. Major Ramiro Valdés, now Minister of Interior and head of all Cuban security forces, was head of G-2 from the first day and his chief deputy was Major "Red Beard" Pineiro. Both are Communists.

After the July expulsion of President Urrutia, the extremists began acquiring new positions. Major Guevara returned from his trip to become head of the Industrialization Department of the Agrarian Institute. In fact, he was the chief of the national economy; his rise was an indication of which way Cuba was moving.

VII

What was perhaps the final turning-point in the leftward swing of the revolution came in October; it marked the virtual extinction of the moderates and had a powerful assist from the United States.

On October 9, Cuba dispatched a note to Washington protesting the flights over the island of clandestine aircraft based in Florida. On October 11, one plane dropped three bombs on a sugar mill in Pinar del Río. Then, on October 22, as Premier Castro drove to the Havana Hilton Hotel to address 2,000 members of the American Society of Travel Agents—a meeting that was partly prompted by a desire to set Cuban-American relations on a more reasonable foot-ing—Major Díaz Lanz flew a B-25 bomber over Havana, dropping leaflets and, according to the Cubans, several bombs. There were dead and wounded as Cuban troops fired machineguns in a flat trajectory over the city.

The same evening, a crowd armed with anti-American posters marched on the modernistic United States Embassy on Malecón Drive to protest the raid. Castro went on tele-vision and charged that the attacking aircraft came from the United States. Once again Castro was handed a perfect pretext for assailing the United States, and again the mod-erates were dealt a blow. Bitterly they asked how it was that the United States could not control its own airfields. The State Department's lame explanation that it knew nothing about the flight did little to salvage the situation, nor did the strange request by Roy R. Rubottom, Jr., Assistant Sec-retary of State for Inter-American Affairs, that the Inter-American Peace Commission investigate the clandestine flights.

Coincidentally, on the morning before the raid, Castro had rushed to Camaguey to arrest Major Huber Matos, the military commander of the province, on charges of trea-son. Matos, who had been one of the leading rebel chiefs in Oriente Province during the war, had resigned from the army in protest against communist infiltration of the mili-tary. In a speech to the officers of his garrison before sending in his resignation, Major Matos said that he had repeatedly brought up the subject of communism with Castro, but that despite the Premier's promises, nothing had been done to end infiltration.

The Matos arrest marked Castro's open espousal of the policy of equating anticommunism with treason. At a trial during which Castro acting as prosecutor, delivered a seven-hour speech, Major Matos was sentenced to thirty years in prison.

A purge swiftly followed. Late in November, Castro pruned out the moderates from his cabinet, Major Guevara succeeding the respected Felipe Pazos as president of the National Bank. At this time Manuel Ray resigned as Min-ister of Public works. During a stormy cabinet session, Edu-cation Minister Hart demanded that Finance Minister Rufo López Fresquet be sent to La Cabaña and executed. Castro was not prepared to go quite that far, and López Fresquet was allowed to remain in the government, although he lost all power to Major Guevara. A few evenings later, López Fresquet told a friend at home that Castro had become "a maniac, a dictator." But he said he would stay on as minister as long as he could because he felt he might still exercise a modicum of restraining influence.

A few weeks earlier, Major Augusto Martínez Sánchéz, a fiery extremist, had become Minister of Labor and played a key role in bringing the Cuban Labor Federation under communist control. David Salvador, president of the Federation, was deprived of real power as two communist leaders, Jesús Soto and José María de la Aguillera, took over effective control.

By now a chorus of attacks on the United States rose daily as government radio stations poured invectives on the Yankee imperialists. The official newspapers ridiculed United States protest notes. Ambassador Bonsal had to wait two months for an appointment with Castro, who later recounted with delight how he had humiliated the envoy by keeping him waiting.

In November the Agrarian Institute seized the cattle land of the King Ranch Company in Camaguey, the first important United States property taken over since the Telephone Company was "intervened" in January. In December the first "counterrevolutionary" trial was held in Pinar del Río with the sentencing of an American pilot and a young Cuban for leading a guerrilla force in Sierra del Organo. The prosecutor and the defense attorney vied with each other in attacks on the United States (but the defense lawyer was soon jailed himself).

In 1959, as "The Year of the Revolution" drew to a close, it was apparent that an abyss had opened between Cuba and the United States. The pulse of events had acquired a rhythm that could no longer be easily altered; the tragedy had to run its quickening collision course.

After ridiculing United States announcements that security measures were being taken to prevent clandestine flights, Castro began talking earnestly about an invasion from the United States. On December 17, he predicted that in 1960 his followers would have "to defend the revolution with weapons at hand." The warning sounded like half prophecy, half wishful-thinking. Although no decision had yet been made by the Eisenhower Administration to organize an invasion, Castro had evidently become aware that such a step was bound to come sooner or later. His sense of history and understanding of revolutionary dynamics made him realize long before Eisenhower himself that there was no other way left but an armed clash.

At year's end, the mood in Cuba recalled the advent of

26

The Terror in the French Revolution. The Girondins were down; the Jacobins were mobilizing the masses into a "sansculottic" army. Four days before Christmas, Castro called on his people to organize a massive informer system, crying, "You men and women must do the job—watch for the counterrevolutionaries." And in the streets of Havana, the chant of *"Pa-re-dón, Pa-re-don"* (To the Wall!) sounded like a grim dirge to those who had dared hope the Cuban revolution would elude dictatorial patterns of the past.

CHAPTER TWO

▷ THE BEWILDERED GIANT

Draw back the curtain of your memory to December 1958. The concerns of the day, in a generally prosperous and contented America, were with a newspaper strike in New York City, with a scrap in the Senate over the election of Everett McKinley Dirksen as Republican Minority Leader, with what Senator Humphrey had said to Mr. Khrushchev during a eight-hour interview, with a new book entitled *Doctor Zhivago* that had first been published in Italy, and with a rude, hirsute and publicity-itchy group of writers who called themselves Beat.

America then had little direct contact with what J. L. Talmon has called political messianism, that blend of democratic rhetoric, testy nationalism and Popular Front-vintage Marxism rising in hungry corners of the world. Names like Sékou Touré, General Kassem, Patrice Lumumba and Cheddi Jagan, were either unknown or dimly remembered. This lack of contact was especially true for Latin America. In May 1958, Vice President Nixon made his disastrous trip to South America, but after the outrage subsided, so did the concern in Washington. In December 1958, a meeting of the "Committee of Twenty-One" was held in Washington to discuss Operation Pan America, a program urged by the Brazilians after the Nixon debacle in order to unite the hemisphere on a massive development program. When Douglas Dillon, the United States representative, first addressed the Committee he neglected to mention either Brazil or Operation Pan America. The chill was completed when the United States said that it opposed long-term multilateral programs and favored a piece-meal approach. Washington was not interested in doing too much for its restive neighbors.

For generations, North Americans had been lulled by a kind of Maginot Line psychology about hemisphere relations. The Monroe Doctrine, the inter-American system, the Pan American movement, the Good Neighbor Policy, these terms were like comforting anodynes to an indifferent giant.

Indeed, in all the lofty rhetoric devoted to Pan Americanism, there was little realization that a different political philosophy animated Latin America. The prophet of democracy in North America was John Locke, stout friend of property, stability and limited government. In Latin America the apostle was Jean-Jacques Rousseau, the Frenchman who influenced hemisphere rebels from the day of Simón Bolívar. Indeed, much of the American reaction to the Cuban Revolution was like that of the horrified Whigs to the Jacobin terror.

If Marx provided the New Testament to Latin American radicals, it is not too much to say that Rousseau provides the Old. *The Social Contract* asserts: "In order then that the social compact may not be an empty formula it tacitly includes the undertaking . . . that whoever refuses to obey the general will shall be compelled to do so by the whole body. This means nothing less than that he will be forced to be free."

"Our will is the general will," announced Rousseau's armed disciple, Robespierre. "They say that terrorism is the resort of despotic government. Is our government then like despotism? Yes, as the sword that flashes in the hand of the hero of liberty is like that with which the satellites of tyranny are armed. . . . The government of the Revolution is the despotism of liberty against tyranny."

Talk like this puzzles and distresses those who see democracy as a neat system of laws and elections, and when it came from a bearded rebel in Havana the reaction was immediately negative. The United States was about to get a costly education in what a messianic revolution can mean.

II

In the beginning, as usual, there was confusion.

On New Year's morning, 1959, President Eisenhower was vacationing in Gettysburg when the news came that Fulgencio Batista had fled Cuba. State Department officials were in anxious consultation, trying to figure out what was going on in Cuba. It was curious but true that the mighty United States knew more about the political ferment in New Delhi or Accra than it did about events on an island "only" —as we were to be frequently informed—90 miles away from Florida.

Batista didn't fall; he collapsed. His army wasn't really beaten; it was eroded away by corruption, low morale and staggeringly incompetent leadership. But up until the eve of Castro's triumph, State Department officials were mesmerized by the statistics—an army of about 40,000, presumably well-equipped and trained, versus a ragtag guerrilla band, holed in the mountains, that probably never numbered much more than 1,000. Indeed, the day before Batista's flight, a news agency solemnly reported that the Cuban army had "won" the battle of Santa Clara.

United States policy concerning Cuba, such as it was (the late John Foster Dulles was frankly bored by Latin America during his tenure as Secretary of State), was based on the assumption that the army in Cuba would serve as a brake against a swing to the far left. Tentative, and awkward efforts had been made during 1958 to try to persuade President Batista to step aside, but the policy was pursued without much sense of urgency or clear direction. It didn't help that our man in Havana, Ambassador Earl E. T. Smith, a genial amateur diplomat on his first assignment, was several degrees warmer to the Batista regime than the ranking inter-American officials at the State Department.

The embarrassed ambivalence of American policy was especially marked after March 15, 1958, when the United States placed an embargo on the shipment of arms to Cuba—a tacit recognition that a civil war was in process. But at the same time that arms were withheld, a U.S. Military Mission was stationed in Havana, helping to train one side in the civil war. Thus Washington was simultaneously embracing and disengaging from Batista, persuading all sides in Cuba that America was playing a slippery game.

Ambassador Smith, an affable sportsman who knew neither Spanish nor revolutions, did little to clear up the ambiguity. In 1957, when Mr. Smith first came to Cuba, he created a brief sensation by expressing outrage at the brutality of Batista policy in battering women demonstrators in Santiago. But unaccountably, Mr. Smith later came to the conclusion that President Batista was not such a bad fellow after all. In March 1958, he tried to dissuade leaders of the civic resistance in Havana from issuing a statement calling for Batista's resignation. The doctors, lawyers

29

and Rotary Club members who composed the civic resistance were furious with Mr. Smith's paternal meddling. The Ambassador's view was that an election would clear the whole matter up. Perhaps his advice was responsible for one of Mr. Dulles' rare visits to a Latin American diplomatic reception. The United States Secretary of State appeared at a Cuban embassy reception only two days before a fixed election was held in Cuba, on November 2. The personal appearance of Mr. Dulles, widely reported on the front pages of the Cuban press, was thought to signify American approval of a bayonet-backed vote.

Suddenly, on New Year's morning, the Batista regime blew apart, like a rickety movie set leveled by a hurricane. Unexpectedly, the State Department found itself confronted by Fidel Castro, who was advancing on Havana in a tumult of excitement.

Who was Castro? What did he believe? No one in Washington was quite sure, and the State Department was frankly hoping for the best. There was little else to be done. Once, Department officials had suggested that contact be made with Castro in his Sierra Maestre headquarters; for obscure reasons, the CIA did not see fit to follow through. Indeed, Ambassador Smith frowned on those newsmen who tried to find out what was on Castro's mind by going to see him. An attempt had also been made, earlier in 1958, to put the Department directly in touch with Castro's choice for President, Judge Manuel Urrutia, who was then in exile in New York. The suggestion was politely brushed aside, although the Department did have informal contact with other Castro spokesmen.

Thus, as 1959 began, Washington looked on apprehensively as an absolute stranger took control of an island which North Americans had come to regard as a kind of extra state. Possibly this lack of comprehension helps to explain the sad little playlet in Washington involving an Ambassador's dog.

III

The dog belonged to Nicolas Arroyo, Batista's envoy to Washington, an architect who was popular with the Capital's social set. Mr. Arroyo was Ambassador until, at 4 a.m. on New Year's morning, Ernesto Betancourt was awakened in Washington by a telephone call. Betancourt, who was then Castro's registered representative in the Capital, heard the excited voice of a friend in Havana telling him that Batista had taken flight.

By 7 a.m., the Cuban Embassy on 16th Street was in rebel hands. Arroyo was still holidaying in New York when he learned that his government was no more. In accordance with a prepared plan, the Embassy was taken over by the Minister, Emilio Pando, whose sympathies had been with the opposition.

That afternoon, amid quiet celebrations of the tyrant's fall, Arthur Gardner, a former American Ambassador in Havana who held Batista in high esteem, contacted the Embassy on Arroyo's behalf. Could the diplomat reclaim his personal belongings? Pando and Betancourt agreed that his personal effects could be removed, but no official papers or property.

Sometime during the next 48 hours, Betancourt received a call from the State Department. Would Dr. Pando and Dr. Felipe Pazos (perhaps the most eminent Cuban exile living in Washington) come to the Department for a visit? There was hurried speculation among the Cubans. Was the United States going to extend congratulations to victorious insurgents? Was there significance in the call?

Shortly thereafter, Drs. Pando and Pazos went to the State Department where they were greeted by, among others, Roy R. Rubottom, then Assistant Secretary for Inter-American Affairs, and Chief of Protocol Wiley Buchanan. But as the meeting developed, the Cubans were made to feel that its primary purpose was to appeal for consideration for the ex-Ambassador, especially to see if something could be done to return Mrs. Arroyo's dresses and the Ambassador's dog.

This was the first official encounter between the agents of a revolutionary regime and the State Department. In Havana, the theme was very much the same. Before Castro arrived in the capital, Havana was under the control of Colonel Ramón Barquin, a gallant democrat who had been imprisoned by Batista for organizing a military coup against the dictatorship. Barquin received two phone calls from Ambassador Smith during the first days of Havana's liberation. The first was a request that Colonel Barquin assure safe exit to Porfirio Rubirosa, the Dominican playboy who was then Trujillo's Ambassador to Batista. The second call was to beseech Colonel Barquin to guarantee the safety of the hundreds of Batistianos who had taken asylum in foreign embassies.

Thus, beginning in January 1959, Cuba and the United

31

States were like dancers continually stepping on each other's feet, because one partner was attempting a stately waltz while the other was lost in the rhapsody of a cha-cha-cha.

IV

"Blood bath," "drumhead justice," "kangaroo courts"—these were the words that blew through the headlines in the next phase of Cuban-American relations. Members of Congress and editorial writers, many of whom had evinced a remarkable stoic detachment about atrocities committed by the Batista dictatorship, were suddenly aroused by the execution of Batista henchmen by revolutionary firing squads.

To the detached outsider, unaware of the deep emotional currents in Cuba, the mass executions were morally repelling and procedurally indefensible. The summary courts-martial were based on an assumption of guilt, conducted in an atmosphere of hysteria, and patently aimed at extracting an eye for an eye. To those accustomed to Anglo-Saxon justice, it was repulsive to see a defendant tried in a sports arena. No less distressing was the disregard for double jeopardy; when a group of Batista fliers was absolved by a Havana court, a second trial was ordered and they were conveniently found guilty.

Hence the news that Cuba was beginning a hopeful revolution was lost under an avalanche of headlines on mass executions. On January 12, Senator Wayne Morse deplored the "blood baths" in Cuba; he was joined three days later by Congressman Wayne L. Hays, who was quick to urge a trade embargo against the island, and by Congressman Emanuel Celler, who asked the Administration to "publicly express horror" and have the matter placed before the United Nations.

To Cubans, moderates as well as radicals, the proprietary tone of the congressional lectures was incomprehensible. The "war criminals" had been convicted in the public mind before the trials began—and it was regarded as justice, in the Spanish, Indian and Afro-Cuban sense of cruel justice and deserved bloody retribution. The defendants were members of the Batista police and army, and many if not most had atrocious records of murder and torture against oppositionists. Cubans were amazed that some who were so righteously shocked by trials held under the full glare of publicity had not evinced similar shock during the Batista years. How come, they asked, American Congressmen and editorial writers had not protested against the gouging of eyes, the cutting of testicles and the slicing of women's breasts in the Batista jails? How come nothing was said when every morning the people of Santiago found their sons, husbands and brothers dead and mutilated in doorways and public squares? Why had the deaths of thousands of persons under the Batista regime been accepted in silence while American tourists gaily flocked to Havana's casinos and nightclubs?

To Castro himself, the criticism was intolerable. On his way to a Rotary Club luncheon, Castro passed through the lobby of the Havana Hilton Hotel. Several reporters, in a bantering mood, needled Castro about the criticism. In an impulsive aside, Castro retorted that "200,000 gringos will die" if the United States should send the Marines—a suggestion that no one was remotely considering.

Thus at the outset the note of hysterical hyperbole was established—a note peculiarly liable to amplification in the megaphone of the press. Reporters were quick to seize the extravagant statement and pump it into a "hard lead" that left the impression that a madman was ranting. But if the reporters were too eager to make a headline, it ought to be added that the bait was planted by Castro himself.

In the first, euphoric days of the revolution, the American press served as a distorting lens. The transfiguring sense of rebirth, the notable civic discipline in Havana, the idealistic fervor of young men suddenly thrust into power—these aspects of the Cuban upheaval did not fit so easily into the wire-service formula of what constitutes news.

Moreover, the very proximity and history of Cuba brought into play a double standard in the United States akin to the anti-Western bias for which the neutralist nations are condemned. Two years later, there was a *coup d'état* in South Korea that brought fervid young anticommunist military officers into power. There were shootings and jailings in South Korea too, a country in which the United States had more direct political responsibility than it had in Cuba. No one rose in Congress to propose an embargo, and there was little talk about "blood baths" in Korea. The feeling of outrage, on our part as well as among the neutrals, is conditioned to some extent by one's attitude to the political beliefs of the man who is pulling the trigger.

V

The American reaction to the mass trials was overdone, coming with special ill-grace from a country that had evinced a massive disinterest about the plight of the Cuban people under Batista—and that showed similar disinterest about other Latin American peoples under dictatorial regimes. But to be critical is not to engage in excessive self-flagellation. Despite the recriminations, considerable good will toward the Cuban revolution was also evident. When Castro came to the United States on an unofficial visit in April, there seemed to be a chance to repair the damage.

The circumstances of the visit were odd but apt. Castro had been invited by the American Society of Newspaper Editors—throughout, the press has served as the chorus in the tragedy. Although the State Department was caught off balance by the invitation, its spokesmen said that Castro "will assuredly be welcome here." Meanwhile, feelings had been soothed by the exchange of ambassadors that sent Philip Bonsal to Cuba and brought to Washington Dr. Ernesto Dibigo, a dignified and elderly professor of law who had once had Castro as a pupil.

Reporters were anticipating lively copy; the "Maximum Leader" did not disappoint them. After he emerged from his plane at Washington National Airport on April 15, he broke away from his security guards and charged over to greet 1,500 persons lined against the airport fence. This set the tone for his irregular and direct personal diplomacy.

The day after his arrival, he lunched with Secretary of State Christian Herter, who met the visitor in the lobby of the Statler Hotel, a procedure that was later criticized for its lack of warmth and dignity (President Eisenhower found it convenient to be out of town when the controversial guest arrived). The wariness existed, but Castro went far on April 17 to dispel suspicion. He spoke at the ASNE banquet before an audience that was predominantly skeptical, if not downright hostile. The effect of his eloquence is suggested by Edward T. Folliard's report in the Washington *Post*:

> Fidel Castro, Prime Minister of Cuba, wrestled bravely with the English language for 2 hours and 15 minutes before the American Society of Newspaper Editors yesterday. To judge from the applause, he scored a victory in the public relations field. . . .
>
> Prime Minister Castro, a big, broad-shouldered fellow of 32 in an olive green uniform, open at the throat below his beard, and with a star on each shoulder, didn't talk like a Communist or a dictator. He spoke for a free press and for all the other freedoms asso-

34

ciated with true democracy. He welcomed American industrial investment in Cuba and guaranteed that it would be safe.

The editors were especially impressed by Castro's explicit denial that he was leading a communist revolution and by his explicit statements on freedom of the press. "The first thing dictators do," he affirmed with prophetic accuracy, "is to finish the free press and establish censorship. There is no doubt that the free press is the worst enemy of dictatorship."

During the next days, the era of good feeling continued. He appeared before the Senate Foreign Relations Committee and was asked: "What is your connection with communism." "None," was the reply. After the closed session, Alabama's Senator John Sparkman said that Castro "made a very favorable impression, I'll say frankly." Congressman James G. Fulton of Pennsylvania allowed that he had been "neutral and suspicious" but was now Castro's *"nuevo amigo."* Florida's Senator George Smathers, esteemed in the upper chamber as something of an expert on Cuban matters, said that he thought Castro personally was a "good man" but had doubts about others in the government.

In this instance, Mr. Smathers had a point. As the American tour continued, with frenetic stopovers at Princeton University, New York City and Harvard University, the applause increased—and so did the telephone calls from Havana. Each night, Cubans who accompanied Castro relate, Brother Raúl was on the phone needling, cajoling, scolding —saying, in effect, "Fidel, are you selling out to the Yankees? That's what people are thinking back home." During his tour, Castro was surrounded by the eminent moderates in his government, men who were known and respected in Washington. But none of these figures had the personal link to Castro that the sharing of mutual hardship forges. His moderate advisers were for the most part beardless; the procommunist wing of the revolution, exemplified by brother Raúl and "Ché" Guevara, had a hold on part of Fidel's being; they had fought together as soldiers in the Sierra, where common peril made strangers into brothers, if not comrades.

Thus, when Castro was in Canada, Raúl urged him to cut his trip short and arrange a meeting in Houston, Texas. Cuban-based guerrilla forces were active in the Caribbean, and the first outcries against the Castro revolution's export policies could be heard. Fidel assented; the voice from the

35

mountains, then as later, prevailed over the calm arguments of the moderates.

VI

Was there really a chance, during the April visit, for the United States to make itself a partner in the Cuban revolution? The possibility has tantalized from the moment Cuban-American relations sank into the maelstrom. Even President Kennedy is on record as wondering whether "Castro would have taken a more rational course had the United States not backed the dictator Batista so long and so uncritically, and had it given the fiery young rebel a warmer welcome in his hour of triumph, especially on his trip to this country...." (*Strategy of Peace*, 1960). Mr. Kennedy confessed that he was not sure; his hesitation is shared by many liberal-minded Americans.

No one can know for certain what might have happened *if*... still, it does seem plausible to contend that there was no real chance for a settlement, even if the United States had tried to clasp Castro to its bosom. Whether or not Castro was telling the truth when he said on December 2, 1961, that he had deliberately disguised his radical views during the formative period of his revolution, his temperament and ambition were such that a real accommodation with his government was never very likely.

Those who saw Castro at short range during his American trip retain vivid mental snapshots of the "Maximum Leader." His was the carriage of a proud, vain, stubborn, and endlessly ambitious leader. Whether he was squatting on his haunches in an intense debate, or whether he was solemnly expounding his views to high-school students in front of the Embassy, he accepted an attentive audience as his due. He could speak with the patient eloquence of a teacher, but the premise invariably was that only the listener had anything to learn. For a leader who continually stressed that his revolution was for the humble, he showed an imperious lack of humility in deciding what the humble ought to want.

Thus the first trait that made any settlement unlikely was pride. Castro was all too familiar with the pattern of past Cuban history, in which a new *caudillo* would certify his claim to power by concluding a deal with American proconsuls in Cuba and by making a pilgrimage to Washington, with its attendant rewards for good behavior. "It is possible," Fidel said to the newspaper editors, "many

36

people believed we were coming here for money. I wish to explain that we didn't come for money. You should not think of our country as a beggar."

Castro instructed his subordinates to ask for no immediate aid, but his advisers did discuss possible aid programs in a general way with U.S. officials. The tone of the conversations was cautious but optimistic. Minister of Finance Rufo López Fresquet assured Americans that the revolution was taking a hopeful course and that existing friction could be ameliorated. Felipe Pazos, head of the National Bank, explained that Castro was still in the "Moncada Barracks" phase of economic thinking. First, Pazos contended, Castro tried to unseat Batista by a wild, frontal attack on the Moncada Barracks in Santiago in 1953—then he went to the Sierra Maestra for a longer, more patient seige. "Castro is still attacking economic problems the way he attacked Moncada," Pazos said. "We're hoping that he will go into the Sierra soon."

There was pride, fierce ambition and the gulf between a radical leader in the messianic tradition and a stand-pat Administration that was afraid to take a chance in dealing with a controversial fellow. Unlike Great Britain, which had been tutored generations ago by the Irish, the United States was not used to dealing with rebels in a nearby country that Washington comfortably regarded as part of its "back yard." And whatever tragic flaws Castro possessed, his driving sense of social justice was authentic. If he had been merely an *ersatz* idealist, his regime would have been in the Peronista tradition—strong on words, weak on deeds. Precisely because Castro was able to communicate the sincerity of his concern he became a hero to the humble from Argentina to Mexico. If Castro had been wholly a villainous cynic, there would be no tragedy in the tale that we are trying to relate.

Whether Castro, at the time of his visit, was a communist is a moot point. But the evidence suggests that he didn't know what he was, except that he was a radical revolutionary—notwithstanding his subsequent hints that all along his road was clear. Vice President Nixon has reportedly taken credit for prescience in writing a memorandum, after his lunch with Castro, asserting that the Cuban was either a Party member or hopelessly naïve about communism. But curiously, the same day that Castro dined with Nixon, he returned to the Cuban Embassy and woke several of his aides who were sleeping on the third floor. He was excited and voluble. According to those present, he said he was worried about two threats to the Cuban revolution—that it would be discredited by the mass executions or by communist infiltration. Possibly his concern was genuine. A few days later, Castro dispatched "Ché" Guevara on a goodwill mission to the neutralist world, thus taking from Cuba the shrewdest of the left-wing intellectuals in his guerrilla group. And, upon his return to Cuba, the executions stopped. In any event, the true facts will remain stuff for debate for years to come.

VII

During the next months, there was a breathing space, interrupted by spasms of controversy. Fidel Castro fortified the impression in Washington that he was well-intentioned but headstrong when he made a flying visit to an economic conference in Buenos Aires and proposed that the United States grant Latin America $30 billion over a ten-year period. (The figure was dismissed as preposterous, but two years later Washington itself was talking about a decade-long program involving $20 billion in U.S. aid, loans for international agencies, private investment and help from Europe.)

If the countries had been given a chance to relax, possibly relations might have normalized. But there were determined groups doing their best to bring out the worst in leaders of both countries. In Cuba, as we have seen, there was an implacably anti-American wing of the Castro regime; at the other extreme were the Batistianos who had fled to Florida and who were in a strategic position to roil the waters.

There was an almost dialectical relationship between the antithetical positions. Each needed the other to keep alive the sense of crisis. To consolidate their hold on Cuba, and on Castro, the Jacobins on the left needed to play upon popular passions by building up the counterrevolutionary threat. For their part, the Batista exiles were keenly aware that their only hope for returning to Cuba lay in an act of intervention by the United States. Both factions, for their own reasons, were intent upon prying apart Castro's Cuba and Eisenhower's America; history testifies to their success.

The various controversies over the clandestine flights, the Díaz Lanz testimony and the agrarian reform have already been outlined. Strangely, just as in the Katanga controversy in December 1961, Senators James O. Eastland and Thomas J. Dodd demonstrated how two legislators can help undercut official policy. Both used the Senate Internal Security Subcommittee as a kind of free-lance foreign office by extending status and recognition to Castro's foes, of whatever stripe.

Caught in the middle were the impotent moderates. Ambassador Dibigo, in Washington, spoke privately to one of the authors in tones of chagrin and dismay. He recalled that his Embassy had tipped off the Cuban desk of the State Department that there were rumors about a B-25 that had been mysteriously sold in the Southwest and was waiting to be flown in a Florida airfield. The tip came to nothing and the plane was later flown by Major Díaz Lanz in his October raid on Havana. Ambassador Dihigo said that it was difficult to explain to his government why Cuba could not even purchase a trainer jet from the United States because of an arms embargo placed on the Caribbean by Washington. How, he asked, can the young rebels in Havana understand why the United States neither prevents the clandestine flights nor permits Cuba to buy planes to defend itself?

Equally baffled was another well-meaning moderate, President Eisenhower. Asked at his October 28 news conference what he thought was "eating" Fidel Castro, the President replied:

I have no—no idea of discussing possible motivations of a man, what he is really doing, and certainly I am not qualified to go into such abstruse and difficult subjects as that. I do feel this: Here is a country that you believe, on the basis of our history, would be one of our real friends. . . . It would seem to make a puzzling matter to figure just exactly why the Cubans would now be, and the Cuban government, would be so unhappy, when, after all, their principal market is right here . . . I don't know exactly what the difficulty is.

Thus the "Year of the Revolution," which had begun with timid expressions of hope, ended in a spree of confiscations, angry diplomatic notes and splenetic threats. In the Cuban view, as it was assiduously shaped by Castro propaganda, the United States was sheltering Batista "war criminals," allowing bombing attacks on Cuba, and threatening to wreck the agrarian reform. Seen from North America, the Cubans were irrationally angry about small things—i.e. clandestine flights—and dangerously blind about big things—i.e.

39

the menace of communism and the need properly to compensate expropriated land-owners.

A stream of protest notes was directed at Havana concerning land seizures. On October 14, a "firm and gentle" note was sent advising Cuba to avert an impending crisis. "If Fidel Castro takes time out to read the note," reported Edwin A. Lahey of the Chicago *Daily News*, "he will get the clear implication that Cuba will get rough treatment from Congress next year unless it begins some serious talks with the State Department on the problems of American sugar and other properties in Cuba."

On November 29, Castro received further paternal advice from Senator Allen J. Ellender, chairman of the Senate Agriculture Committee and a warm admirer of the Trujillo regime in the Dominican Republic. Mr. Ellender said simply that Congress might retaliate against Cuban confiscation by slashing the island's share of the United States sugar market. The ground was being seeded for the next phase of Cuban-American relations during "The Year of the Agrarian Reform."

CHAPTER THREE

⇨ CRUCIBLE OF REVOLT

With the advent of the New Year in Cuba—the second year of the revolution—Cuban-American relations were charting a sharp downward line on the graph. But not quite a straight line; in the first three or four months of 1960, Fidel Castro alternated smiles and frowns at the United States. It was as if the Premier were deliberately trying to create the impression of systematic persecution by the United States in disregard of Cuba's offers to improve relations.

Even if Castro were really sincere in his protestations that he wished to arrive at an accommodation with Washington—and his own words subsequently suggested that this was never his intent—the momentum of deterioration was too swift to be stopped.

Once again, the United States abetted Castro's maneuvers by failing to halt the constant flights from Florida by light aircraft dropping bombs and incendiary devices on Cuba's sugar fields just as the harvest was beginning. Castro was thus able to claim that the United States was responding to his overtures with acts of aggression tolerated by officials in Washington.

Why did the United States display such impotent incompetence in blocking the flights? Why was corrective legal action so tardy? The answer is not easy to find; the flights were a profound disservice to Washington and had the grievous effect of turning the Cuban people against the United States, an objective that Castro presumably had in mind.

Indeed, the flights were so useful to Castro that there is evidence that the Havana regime arranged some of the flights deliberately as a way of discrediting the United States as an aggressor. An investigation by the Department of Justice and a Federal Grand Jury in Miami in April 1960 produced evidence that several Cuban agents, including a consul in Miami, had unexplained contacts with certain free-lance American fliers. Conclusive evidence of "auto-aggression" was never really obtained; those who could tell the full story were either dead or otherwise unable to talk. But the circumstantial evidence is impressive.

On February 19, a plane exploded in the air over the España sugar mills in Las Villas Province. Its pilot, an American named Robert Ellis Frost, was killed. This was followed on March 22 by a more intriguing incident when Cuban troops near Matanzas shot down a plane carrying two Americans, William L. Schergales and Howard Rund· quist. An American vice-consul in Havana somehow succeeded in visiting Schergales at the Matanzas Hospital, where the pilot was being held, and obtained from him what the State Department described as an affidavit that he had been paid by the Cuban regime to make the flight. Schergales named Juan Orta, head of Dr. Castro's Executive Office, as the man who arranged the flight. Although the United States Government repeatedly asked for the extradition of Schergales and Rundquist for trial in Miami after their indictment by the Grand Jury, no reply was ever given. The fliers had vanished in Cuba. Orta, who broke with Castro early in 1961, is in asylum in the Venezuelan Embassy in Havana and, at the time of this writing, cannot shed any light on the strange episode.

However, even without these incidents, Cuban-American relations were worsening by the day. Late in January, Washington recalled Ambassador Bonsal from Havana in

41

response to the "insulting" treatment of the United States by Cuba's official propaganda. At the same time that Castro and his Foreign Minister, Raúl Roa, were proposing negotiations, the Cuban radio and press were venting wild attacks on the United States. Children in the paramilitary Juvenile Patrols were taught marching songs about the Yankees being unable to cope with Castro and about Eisenhower being a stupid old man.

On February 14, visiting Soviet Deputy Premier Anastas Mikoyan signed a trade agreement with Castro under which Russia would buy a million tons of sugar a year for five years and grant Cuba $100,000,000 in credits. Cuba had sold sugar to the Soviet Union even under the Batista regime, but the pact with Mikoyan was seen by Washington as a first step in shifting Cuba's economic relationship to the Russian bloc.

Nine days later, the Castro regime sent an unexpected note to the United States suggesting negotiations on outstanding matters, but with the proviso that no executive or legislative action that could be considered as detrimental to Cuba would be taken by America during the talks. The implication, as understood in Washington, was that the United States could engage in no steps to protect its interests no matter what the Cubans did in the course of what could be endlessly protracted negotiations. Nothing came of the Cuban offer, but it was a skillful play for the gallery because it made the United States seem as if it were only willing to negotiate holding a club behind its back.

On March 6, the entire city of Havana was shaken by a deafening explosion on the French munitions ship *La Coubre*, whose hold contained military supplies bought by the Cubans in Belgium. About seventy persons were killed in the waterfront carnage. Castro immediately charged that the United States was behind the explosion, and his newspaper, *Revolución*, chimed in with the baffling comment that the alleged sabotage was an excuse for intervention. Although Castro subsequently backtracked from his initial accusation, his propaganda machine hammered relentlessly on the theme of American sabotage. A special horror booklet was produced by the Foreign Ministry to be circulated throughout the world, implying that the United States was indeed guilty of the dockside massacre.

It is impossible to tell what had set off the explosion, but the charge of American sabotage is highly improbable. Whatever the cause, experts blamed Cuban authorities for the grave error of tying up a munitions ship alongside a wharf for unloading. Normally, ships carrying explosives are anchored in the middle of the harbor and unloaded by lighters.

In any event, the blowing up of *La Coubre* exploded what was left of the chance for improving relations between Castro and the United States. The revolutionary regime began taking over United States property along with land and industry owned by Cuban interests. The original expectation had been that United States companies would lose their land under the provisions of the Agrarian Reform Law, and that in time the American-owned utilities would be taken over. But now the regime began to move indiscriminately to seize every type of property. On March 12, the first three United States-owned sugar mills were taken. Simultaneously, the huge nickel plant of the Moa Mining Company in Oriente Province, where Castro's rebels were allowed to hide during the war against Batista, was "intervened," the legal step preceding outright nationalization. The company's worth was $75,000,000, and the seizure accounted for the largest slice of United States investment out of the $1,000,000,000 or so seized until that time.

II

That Cuba intended to grab all United States property sooner or later was presently made clear by Major Ernesto "Ché" Guevara, the president of the National Bank, who always displayed blunt candor in discussing the regime's plans.

In a speech on the televised Popular University program on March 19, Major Guevara announced that "our economic war will be with the great power of the North." In what can be read as a declaration of ideological as well as economic war, Guevara asserted:

. . . To conquer something, we have to take it away from somebody, and it is well to speak clearly and not hide behind concepts that could be misinterpreted. This something that we have to conquer is the sovereignty of the country; it has to be taken away from that somebody who is called the monopoly . . . although monopolies in general have no country, they have at least a common definition: all the monopolies that have been in Cuba, that have profited from the Cuban land, have very close ties with the United States. This is to say that our economic war will be with the great power of the North . . . our road toward

43

liberation will be found in the victory over the monopolies, and concretely over the North American monopolies.

At the same time that Castro and Foreign Minister Roa were still proposing negotiations over the sugar quota and compensation for land seized for the agrarian reform, Major Guevara was already forecasting the takeover of other American property. This throws a different light on the Cuban condition for negotiations, which called for a guarantee that the United States would take no adverse action during the talks.

In fact, Guevara could not have been more explicit in expounding what the Cuban government had in mind. Subsequently, however, Castro managed to create the impression that the wholesale seizure of property after July was merely a retribution for the elimination of the Cuban sugar quota. The Cuban revolutionaries were becoming adept at the art of provoking the adversary into angry reprisals and then shifting the blame to the adversary for having reacted.

In explaining the land reform as part of the revolutionary battle against the "colonialist monopolies"—instead of as a measure to provide justice for the Cuban peasant—Major Guevara had this to say:

We had to hit the most irritating of all the monopolies, the monopoly of the land holdings, to destroy it, to make the land pass to the hands of the people, and then begin the real struggle because this, despite all, was simply the first entry into contact with the two enemies ... The battle will be given now, it will be given in the future, because although the monopolies had here great stretches of land, it is not there the most important ones are; the most important ones are in the chemical industry, in engineering, in petroleum. . . .

During the same speech, which looms in retrospect as one of the milestone utterances of the revolution, Major Guevara also developed the argument that the United States sugar quota system—which brought Cuba about $150,000,000 annually in extra bonus payments over the world market price—was a form of "economic slavery."

He explained that this system forces Cubans to accept customs obligations with the United States under which the island has to spend in imports from the mainland $1.15 for every dollar earned through the bonus arrangement. There-

44

fore, he said, the quota system made $1,000,000,000 pass from Cuban hands into the hands of the "North American monopolies." To begin selling sugar to the Soviet Union, he said, and to buy Soviet oil at prices 33 per cent below United States prices, was to begin to move toward emancipation.

Following the Guevara speech, the United States spent more than three months in formal inquiries to the Cuban government as to whether the Major had indeed been enunciating official policy when he indicated that the Castro regime wanted no part of the sugar quota. The Cubans, not surprisingly, never bothered to reply; Guevara was one of the chief spokesmen of the revolution and nobody was about to negate his words.

This situation led to perhaps the most absurd argument that developed between the two countries. The United States was claiming that the quota was a generous gift to Cuba but it was threatening to take it away—not to punish the island but to "assure" sugar supplies. The Cubans were claiming that the quota was "economic slavery" but they indignantly charged that Washington would be practicing unfair economic warfare if it should take the quota away.

To the extent that it mattered, the United States position was sounder, although the Cubans had legitimate grievances. At the time of Guevara's statement, it is worth stressing, Cubans were still receiving the bonus payments but were no longer spending most of their dollars on the mainland. Guevara had drastically curtailed imports to save hard currency and the United States was officially indignant over his refusal to continue the traditional purchases on the mainland. Thus the bonus system need not have involved "economic slavery" if the Cuban government kept the benefits on the island.

At the same time, there was weight to the Cuban argument that the sugar quota was set unilaterally by Congress, meaning that the island had no direct say on a decision vital to its economy. Yet tariffs were subject to reciprocal negotiations, which meant that the United States could use its leverage to maintain a low-tariff market in Cuba for American exports. And it was also true that the chief purpose of the sugar-quota system was not to "help" Cuba but to protect less efficient producers in the United States. In short, like many economic problems, the sugar was a simple matter of right or wrong only in polemics that were fired back and forth between Havana and Washington.

It was against this background of swiftly worsening relations that the State Department made the debatable decision to send back Ambassador Bonsal. This step was taken against the advice of the entire Embassy staff in Havana. Their opposition was based on the fear that Bonsal's return would be taken as a sign of weakness and would encourage Castro to engage in further humiliation of Americans. Their fears turned out to be justified.

Mr. Bonsal landed in Havana the day after Major Guevara made his "economic warfare" speech and a day before Schergales and Runquist were shot down in Matanzas. The timing of his return could scarcely have been worse. For the next six months, Mr. Bonsal underwent probably the most frustrating and humiliating experience imposed upon an American ambassador. His ordeal included his inability to obtain an appointment with Castro, futile protests to Foreign Minister Roa or his assistants over the arrest of American citizens, seizure of property or propaganda insults hurled at the United States. Embassy officials made increasingly frequent pilgrimages to the headquarters of the G-2 (secret police) in a sickly green villa on Havana's Fifth Avenue to inquire about Americans under arrest. There was seldom valid reason for the detentions and soon United States correspondents in Havana became the favorite target of the sport-shirt attired G-2 agents. A feeling of helplessness infected Americans in Havana as they realized that their government could no longer protect them.

A radical, dynamic revolution has no respect for weakness, or what it thinks to be weakness. The Cuban regime savored the humiliations that Mr. Bonsal and his staff suffered in silence. But here again we run into the pattern of inevitability that trapped American diplomatic efforts. If the United States had taken an aggressively hostile policy, the effect would surely have been to make Castro a martyr and to have strengthened the impression in Latin America that Washington was trying to crush a social revolution. Yet, in practicing the policy of "patience and forebearance," the United States may have advanced its larger Latin American goals, but at the price of encouraging Castro to attempt spectacular new effronteries.

As it was, Bonsal lost all contact with Cuban public opinion that was still strongly supporting Castro. His personal policy was to avoid exposure and conflict, and he was in no position to use his prestige to present Washington's side of the story. When a Havana TV and radio network agreed to let him appear on a program, the Ambassador decided not to do it. He discouraged his aides from sending vigorous statements of the American position to the remaining independent newspapers in Cuba.

One of the last people-to-people ties between the two countries was broken in April when the Rochester baseball team of the International League decided not to play in Havana any more. The local Sugar Kings lost their franchise. Safety of the Rochester players was invoked as the reason, and Castro promptly charged aggression in the sports realm. But a New York ballet group came to Havana at the same time, and dainty ballerinas apparently did not fear to dance where the tough baseball players were loath to tread. For a few more months, however, Cubans enjoyed live TV pickups of baseball games on the mainland and the boxing match in which their compatriot Benny Parets won a world title.

These were the few remaining threads in the fabric of the old relationship, but they could not obscure the size of the vent now dividing the two governments and the two systems. Yet optimists professed to see a chance for a modus vivendi, and Castro occasionally threw them crumbs of encouragement, in between attacks on the United States.

Thus, on March 30, he coupled warnings to Washington that Cuba was not a Guatemala where a revolutionary regime could be overthrown by the CIA, with an offer to send Cuban Ambassador Ernesto Dihigo back to the United States after a lapse of three months, "if they are ready to discuss things on a friendlier basis." But in the same nightlong speech he insisted again that anticommunism was tantamount to counterrevolution, and announced that his regime was not bound by the 1947 inter-American treaty of Reciprocal Assistance signed at Rio de Janeiro.

At the Labor Day celebration on May 1, Castro told a crowd of 500,000 that the United States was preparing an aggression against Cuba through Guatemala and added that the United Fruit Company—his favorite target, along with the State Department and the CIA—was backing it.

On that day, his supporters for the first time burst out publicly in the chant of "Cuba Si, Yankee No," and the United States was thus officially designated the enemy of the revolution. But despite the chorus of hate, Castro again chose to throw out a crumb of encouragement. Four days after his May Day speech, his regime confidentially advised the State Department that José Miró Cardona, the first Premier in the revolutionary government and later Ambassador to Spain, would be sent as the new Ambassador to the United States.

The State Department immediately and hopefully indicated its approval; the American press pointed out that Dr. Miró Cardona was a respected moderate, and the new Ambassador-designate said that he would fly to Washington as soon as possible. It is still unclear why Castro bothered to go through these motions. Dr. Miró Cardona was never given permission to take up his post, and in July he finally broke with the regime to seek asylum in the Argentine Embassy. He later became president of the Cuban Revolutionary Council in whose name the invasion of the Bay of Pigs was launched.

In recalling his fleeting appointment as Ambassador, Dr. Miró Cardona later told of seeing Castro only once on his return from Spain and never being able to secure an appointment as he sat in Havana waiting to go to Washington. In a series of conferences with Ambassador Bonsal, he had established a basis for improved relations and he reported to President Dorticos that the prospects were favorable provided the violent anti-American propaganda in Havana could be halted. Dr. Miró Cardona recounted that Dorticos had given him such assurances. But, he said, a few hours later Castro was again before the TV cameras with another sulphuric attack on the United States.

Three days after asking for diplomatic *agrément* for Dr. Miró Cardona, the Cuban regime established official relations with the Soviet Union and prepared an exchange of ambassadors. The timing looked suspiciously as if Castro were trying to tease Washington.

By then, Soviet bloc technicians were already pouring into Cuba, although they were still staying discreetly out of sight. The Soviet tanker *Vishinsky* had brought the first shipment of Soviet petroleum for a small, government-owned refinery. Cuban officials and newspapers were talking less and less about the regime's equidistant position between East and West, and more and more of friendship for the Soviet Union. After the summit meeting in Paris broke up late in May, Castro's newspaper *Revolución* described Eisenhower as a warmonger and heaped praise on Soviet Premier Khrushchev's performance.

Castro was applying taunting pressure on all fronts; the frayed rope of Cuban-American relations was being pulled taut and was almost ready to snap.

From the dawn of his revolution, Castro saw his movement as one that was not confined to Cuba but that should
be made to spread across Latin America. He foresaw a
hemisphere-wide uprising against the United States and its
influence, and already, early in 1960, a new slogan emerged
proclaiming Cuba as the "Free Territory of the Americas."

In fact, however, even this mission was too modest for
Castro. He began talking of Cuba inspiring revolutions everywhere in the underdeveloped world, and he predicted
that a revolution would ultimately come to the United
States. To encourage this project, Cuban propaganda busied itself spreading leaflets in Spanish and English in the
South of the United States and in New York's Harlem
urging American Negroes to rise against oppression. As an
added fillip, the Cubans made contact with American In-
dians, too; in July 1959 Castro received Mad Bear, an Iro-
quois nationalist, as a guest in Havana.

While the United States was not overly alarmed by these
Castro activities on the mainland (although Washington subsequently grossly underestimated the size and quality of the
Cuban intelligence network in Miami, New York and Washington), it did view with extreme concern the efforts to
"export" the revolution to Latin America. Latin American
masses were evidently receptive to the example of the
sweeping reforms put into effect in Cuba, and the activities
of Castro-sympathizers were creating deep political and
security problems for the moderate governments in the hemisphere.

"We are a bad example for Latin America," Castro and
Guevara kept repeating with visible glee, and Washington
could not agree more. The Cubans had defied the United
States not only in terms of their direct and immediate re-
lationship, but also in terms of carrying the war against
"Yankee imperialism" into the very heart of the hemisphere
to undermine the United States position everywhere in Latin
America.

Their activities in Latin America served the twin objectives of sabotaging the United States influence and of
assuring the Cubans of political support in the already fore-
seeable event that Washington would attempt to organize
diplomatic action against Cuba through the Organization of
American States, or even try for a military solution. But
fundamentally Castro's concentration on Latin America was

designed to underscore the whole rationale of his policy toward the United States: he was engaged in a total war against the "great power of the North" and thrusts against its soft underbelly throughout the restive hemisphere was part of the grand design. The obverse of this policy was that any accommodation with the United States on any terms short of Washington's total acceptance of his position would weaken his revolutionary efforts in Latin America.

Early in the spring of 1960 Castro sent out a delegation of his "26th of July Movement" to tour Latin America. It was headed by Carlos Olivares Sánchez, a communist from Oriente Province who soon after became the Deputy Foreign Minister and the real political power in planning Cuban foreign policy. Foreign Minister Roa, who only a few years before had written a book highly critical of communism, stayed on as the international spokesman for the regime. Late in 1961, Roa made up for his earlier lapse by announcing in a speech that communism was the world's, and Cuba's, "wave of the future." Castro echoed Roa a month later.

The Olivares mission, which stressed only the social-reform aspects of the Cuban revolution and Cuba's friendship for Latin America, was fairly successful. But it failed to persuade any Latin American government to agree to attend a world "hunger conference" of underdeveloped countries that Castro was planning to hold in Havana in the fall of 1960. The conference was never held.

Late in May, President Dorticós, Roa and a group of Cuban military commanders set out on a Latin American tour that immediately became a campaign aimed at depicting the United States as a political, economic and military aggressor against Cuba. In speeches and news conferences, Dorticós hammered on the theme that Cuba was a daily victim of air attacks from the United States against "our cane fields, our industrial plants, and even our capital." Although the anti-Castro flights were continuing despite tightened security measures that had finally been imposed by United States authorities, the Dorticós charges were wildly but deliberately exaggerated. Cuba, on the other hand, was portrayed by its President as free of communism, dedicated to the freedom of the press and enjoying excellent relations with the Roman Catholic Church. At this point, however, the last independent newspaper in Havana had been forced to shut down and Cuban bishops were drafting a pastoral letter against Communist infiltration.

50

For Dorticós, the trip had the effect of lifting him from what was assumed to be a figurehead role to a position of prominence and, ultimately, of considerable personal power. For the United States, it was a grim reminder of the spreading Cuban influence in the hemisphere.

At about the same time, Cuba imported powerful short-wave transmitters from Switzerland and inaugurated regular propaganda programs beamed to Latin America. The central theme of the broadcasts was the evils of "Yankee imperialism."

On July 26, when Castro celebrated the seventh anniversary of his revolutionary movement, a Latin American Youth Congress was held in Havana. The participants were mostly leftist students from all over the hemisphere, and they were subjected to intense anti-American and revolutionary indoctrination. Simultaneously, arrangements were made to bring Latin American students to Cuba regularly on scholarships.

By now Havana was becoming the magnet for the revolutionary left in Latin America. Cheddi Jagan, British Guiana's leftwing Prime Minister, visited Castro and signed a trade agreement. Chile's communist poet, Pablo Neruda, and procommunist Senator Salvador Allende were constant guests in Havana. Guatemala's ex-president Jacobo Arbenz Guzmán, a procommunist ousted by a CIA-aided rebel invasion in 1954, came to live in Cuba. Mexico's leftist ex-President Lázaro Cárdenas was another honored guest. Brazil's Janio Quadros, then a presidential candidate, spent a week in Cuba in April, bringing along Francisco Julião, the head of the pro-Castro Peasant Leagues in the Brazilian Northeast. (The day after Castro announced in December 1961 that he was a Marxist-Leninist, Julião rushed to say that he, too, was a communist.)

American Embassy officials were reporting all these comings and goings in worried telegrams to Washington. But it was again Major Guevara, that advocate of "speaking clearly," who spelled out in full detail what the Cuban revolutionary leadership expected to see happen in Latin America.

In April 1960 he published his manual on "The War of the Guerrillas"—the "General Principles of the Guerrilla Struggle"—setting out in superb detail the tactics and the strategy to be followed in organizing and carrying out a revolution based on peasant and worker support against the armies and the established government.

On the very first page of his essay, Guevara discussed what he called Cuba's contribution "to the mechanics of revolutionary movements in America," and observed that in "underdeveloped South America, the field of the armed struggle must be fundamentally in the countryside."

"It is necessary to demonstrate clearly to the people," he wrote, "the impossibility of maintaining the struggle for social revindications within the framework of a civic contest."

As Washington shuddered, copies of the Guevara handbook of revolution began turning up throughout Latin America, along with other bundles of Cuban propaganda distributed by the Cuban embassies. Castro was now openly fighting the United States from Mexico's Rio Grande to the Argentine Pampas.

V

However, if Castro was thus extending his field of aggressive revolutionary activities beyond Cuba's insular confines, problems were beginning to develop for him right at home. For the first time since his victory in January 1959, organized opposition against his regime was emerging in Cuba, and it no longer was limited to the former soldiers of the Batista government—the *Casquitos*, as they were called, after the Army helmets they had once worn—or other Batista officials whom the revolutionary police had not flushed out.

This nascent opposition included many of Castro's former supporters in the ranks of the rebel army, the "26th of July Movement," Roman Catholic organizations, and other groups. These were disillusioned and embittered moderates who had once risked their lives in the anti-Batista underground in the name of the great principles of freedom and justice that Castro had so convincingly proclaimed from his Sierra Maestra hideout. Now they were seeing Castro opening the gates of the revolution to communist infiltration and gradually turning the revolutionary regime into a monolithic dictatorship. For the first time since Batista's fall, the word began to be whispered in Cuba that a great revolution was being betrayed.

It was surely inevitable that this new breed of rebel would gravitate toward the United States; not because they were necessarily in sympathy with the way in which Washington had handled the Cuban revolution, but because they had no alternative. There was nowhere else to go. It was part of the polarization process; as Castro himself was repeating daily, you had to be with the revolution or against it. There was no middle ground. And because of the very

52

nature of the political gravitational forces at work in Cuba, those who chose to break with the revolution were automatically propelled toward the United States. Thus, for reasons that can best be described as centrifugal, the United States was perforce becoming an active adversary of the Castro regime, perhaps unconsciously abandoning the confused passivity of the first year or so of the revolution.

Since these new anti-Fidelistas themselves refused to be passive about their opposition and at once rushed into conspiracies, whether they were still in Cuba or had already fled to Florida, it was equally inevitable that the United States should forthwith become associated with these efforts. Therefore, like an irreversible engine, the inexorable drive of Cuban-American relations forced Washington to become an active partner in the emerging plots against Castro even before Easter of 1960.

It is difficult to determine precisely whether at this juncture the United States was acting from a political reflex or whether the Eisenhower Administration had already taken the historic decision that Castro had to be smashed at whatever cost, through any means at hand and as soon as possible. If this decision had not yet been taken formally in the early spring of 1960, all the ingredients for the decision were available, and pushed by the events in Cuba, the Administration was moving toward the only solution that appeared in its view to remain.

It is a fascinating historical pursuit to meditate over the extent to which great nations arrive coolly and deliberately at their great decisions—and over the extent to which decisions, even of dubious wisdom, are imposed by circumstances and the pressure of events beyond their control. In the case of Cuba and the United States, the conscious American decision to destroy Castro—whatever the exact point in time it was finally reached—seems to have been a reflex set off by the appearance of the anti-Castro conspiracies and then rationalized into national policy through a too facile inductive process.

As future events were to show, the United States was fated to have its policies again influenced by the driving momentum behind the anti-Castro forces when it allowed itself to be pushed into the folly of the Bay of Pigs invasion.

In any event, there is evidence that early in 1960 the Central Intelligence Agency had surreptitiously established working arrangements with anti-Castro groups in Cuba as well as in Florida. And it was at that time that the CIA committed the grievous error of extending these arrangements to extreme rightist and Batistano groups, despite assurances given at the time by the Eisenhower Administration and subsequently by the Kennedy Administration that the United States would have no dealing with personages, high or low, who were closely identified with the *ancien régime*. This initial political blunder committed by the CIA in the spring of 1960 was to plague it for the next twelve months and to contribute heavily to the failure of the invasion. This decision also marked the inauguration by the CIA of what, in effect, became its independent foreign policy toward Cuba, in cavalier disregard of the thinking in the White House and the State Department.

Thus the CIA established contacts in Miami with pro-Batista organizations and with exile groups whose entire political philosophy was dedicated to the return to the pre-Castro status quo in Cuba. This would mean the scrapping of land reform, the end of other reforms, and the return of all seized property. These factions were placing themselves not only against Castro, but against history; whether or not the CIA operatives were aware that total regression is impossible, their contacts with the rightist factions ran counter to official United States policy, aimed at encouraging social reform in Latin America.

One such organization existing at the time, although it later vanished in the maelstrom of exile politics, was the White Rose, a Miami faction with limited contacts in Cuba. In the early spring of 1960, CIA agents on the island busied themselves with delivering weapons and radio transmitters to the White Rose plotters, presumably to build them up into a sabotage force or the nucleus of a guerrilla operation. It is hard to believe that the CIA seriously expected that a group composed of thoroughly discredited Batistanos could command enough support to overthrow Castro. CIA agents being made to take the risk of being caught while carrying weapons for the White Rose in the trunks of their cars, some with diplomatic licenses, is one of those exercises in foolishness that was to characterize much of the anti-Castro operation.

But the CIA also began to work with democratic anti-Castro organizations that were beginning to emerge in Cuba, and notably with the Movement of Revolutionary Recovery *(Movimiento de Revolucionaria Recuperación)* which was launched clandestinely by a group of former military and civilian supporters of Castro. This was seemingly a more rational step, but later the MRR lost its original identity

54

and became another rightist organization manipulated by the CIA.

In the beginning, the MRR was a "clean" revolutionary organization. Among its founders were three former captains of Castro's rebel army: Jorge Sotús, Higinio "Nino" Díaz and Sergio Sanjenís. Sotús was a young guerrilla leader who was one of the first Castro captains forced out of combat by Raúl Castro because of his opposition to communism in the Sierra Maestra. Nino Díaz, who was to figure prominently in later events, had also fought in the Sierra Maestra, then turned on the Castro brothers because of his anticommunism. Sanjenís had been the chief of intelligence for Havana in the rebel army early in 1959. He resigned when he became aware that the intelligence section had been taken over by the communists.

Castro's intelligence service was alert. Sotús was arrested in Santiago early in 1960; he escaped in December 1960 in a spectacular break from a Havana prison. Sanjenís was arrested with six companions the day before Easter, 1960, after one of his coplotters turned out to be a Castro agent. They were captured hours after Sanjenís in cooperation with CIA agents spirited Nino Díaz into the Guantanamo Navy Base from Havana. Sanjenís was sentenced to twenty years in prison and is believed to be at the Isle of Pines penitentiary where Huber Matos, the former Camagüey army commander, is also held.

The MRR started out as a secret organization composed of former rebel army officers. It also had close connections with young professionals and Roman Catholic youths who were setting up an underground through a Church-based organization known as "Catholic Groupement" (*Agrupción Católica*).

The one Castro opponent who joined the MRR through the Catholic groups was Manuel Artime Buesa. He had been a captain in the rebel army, fought briefly in the Sierra Maestra, and became chief of the Agrarian Reform zone in Oriente Province. He was a gifted orator and a fanatical anticommunist. After breaking with the regime, he fled to Mexico where he wrote a book denouncing Castro for his plan to communize Cuba. Later, he went to Miami to become one of the chiefs of the MRR organization there. It was Artime that the CIA later picked to command the invasion forces.

At Havana University, the anticommunist activities were directed by a third-year law student named Alberto Muller, who had close connections with the Catholic groups and, more loosely, with the MRR. Muller and his supporters engaged in a futile struggle with the Federation of University Students (FEU), where communists already held considerable sway. Early in April, his newspaper, *Trinchera,* was burned and his supporters beaten, and Muller was forced to abandon the University.

The last open gesture by the Muller group was an attempted demonstration at the door of the TV studios of the CMQ network in Havana in favor of Luis Conte Agüero, a popular commentator and biographer of Castro who had delivered a violent public speech a few days earlier accusing Castro of tolerating communist influence. In the ensuing fracas, Conte Agüero, an old friend whom Castro quickly denounced as a traitor, was prevented from entering the station by communist strongarm squads. He later fled Cuba.

All these new anti-Castro groups had contact with the American Embassy in Havana and with CIA operatives who had their headquarters there. Plans were drawn for the smuggling or parachuting of radio transmitters into Cuba for the MRR underground and for the supply of arms. The CIA and the United States Government had thus firmly entered the conspiracy to oust Castro.

The Premier, who had an efficient secret service and considerable political imagination, wasted no time in going on the offensive. On April 22, Castro made a speech asserting that criticism in Washington was part of a "well-prepared and premeditated plan" to create an internal front against the regime. The plan was premeditated but not particularly well-prepared, as events were to show.

Early in April, Castro had to contend with a guerrilla operation in Oriente led by Captain Manuel Beatón, a semiliterate former Sierra Maestra fighter against Batista. Beatón, whose force was mainly made up of his relatives, had no clear political ties. The CIA ignored him, and the MRR, suspicious that the whole movement might be a Castro decoy, refused to support the Beatón operation. Castro brought thousands of regular troops and some of his brand-new militia units to flush out Beatón's tiny force, well aware from his own experience of the dangers of letting a guerrilla operate with impunity. Beatón was finally captured and executed.

Castro had less success, however, with a guerrilla band led by Nino Díaz that was organized at about the same time in the mountains in the Guantánamo area. There are good reasons to believe that Díaz had gone into the hills from Guantánamo Navy base and that the CIA had given him some support. But Díaz could not muster enough men

56

and his guerrillas never had any contact with the Castro forces. Soon thereafter Díaz turned up in Miami, where he linked up with MRR elements.

The MRR had entered the conspiracy in an official way in the first week of April with the publication of a manifesto urging Cubans to take up arms to defend the revolution and democracy. In the eyes of Cubans—and of the CIA —it had become the foremost instrument for bringing about the fall of Castro. But neither the MRR nor the right-wing groups could have hoped to carry out their plans without external help. To provide such help became the mission of the CIA as the Cuban-American relationship moved quietly into a new dimension.

CHAPTER FOUR

▷ THE CHASM OPENS

The first year, "the Year of the Revolution," presented a political problem to the United States Government. But in 1960, "the Year of the Agrarian Reform," the problem was as much psychological. The Furies were loose in Washington and Havana; before the year ended, Castro had seized some $1 billion in American-owned property, and the United States had come to the verge of organizing an invasion of Cuba.

It is not enough to explain the schism in political terms. Peel away the verbiage of dispute and underneath lay a sense of outrage, raw and red, about an ungrateful child spitting in Father's face. For in the Caribbean area, the United States had in some measure acquired an imperial attitude without accepting imperial responsibility.

There is a curious contrast in American relations with Cuba, Puerto Rico and the Philippines—the three territories whose destiny was determined by the Spanish-American War. In the Philippines and Puerto Rico, the United States accepted direct colonial responsibility. The necessary evil of colonial rule was compensated by certain palpable benefits—health, welfare and educational measures, the training of administrative cadres, the encouragement of free institutions. The paradoxical outcome is that the two areas that the United States administered as colonies are today self-governing and essentially friendly—whereas the country nominally freed by the war is a hive of anti-Americanism. Strikingly, all the major parties in Puerto Rico, a self-governing commonwealth, and the Philippines, independent since 1946, are essentially friendly to the United States.

Cuba suffered most of the evils of colonialism but won few of the benefits. The island was, in a sense, an indirect colony, a client state dominated by private United States economic interests. While the Republic possessed the trappings of sovereignty, it enjoyed little of the substance. Until 1934, the Platt Amendment gave the United States power to intercede directly in Cuban affairs; on two occasions the power was used. Even after the Platt Amendment was abrogated, a psychological Platt Amendment remained stamped on the minds of both Cubans and Americans.

The United States had a choice when the Spanish-American War concluded. It could have acquired Cuba as an outright possession, or it could have granted more genuine independence to the island. We did neither, but chose an unsatisfactory course in between—unsatisfactory because it generated the sense of legitimate outrage that Castro was able to exploit and because it left a legacy in the American mind that made it impossible to accept the extravagant form that Cuban nationalism took.

Much of the tension of 1960 can be explained in terms of the very special attitude of the two peoples toward each other. It is suggestive that there was no comparable expression of popular outrage in the United States when Juan Perón of Argentina prodded and nettled the Colossus of the North. Yet Perón's affronts were in some ways as menacing as Castro's. In the midst of a shooting war with the Axis, Perón made Argentina a haven for Nazis and encouraged fifth-column movements throughout the hemisphere. But Argentina is a big country, a distant country, and a country whose sovereign right to misbehave was not in dispute. Certainly there was concern about Perón's peculations, but the alarm was mainly among editorial writers, diplomats and the informed few.

There was no Platt Amendment psychology concerning Argentina. Cuba was different; it was a country that was "ours" to be "lost." At every point, the warp of the past was evident in 1960. In America, the topic of Cuba became a raw nerve that every politician wishing attention could scratch and inflame. In Cuba, the legacy of the past divided Cubans against themselves; because so many islanders acted as puppets and brokers for U.S. business colonialism, Castro was able to discredit even honorable democrats as Yankee stooges. In Florida, the Platt Amendment psychology made itself felt in the curious and unhealthy relationship between exiles and the CIA. An older generation of Cuban leaders had been conditioned to look to Washington as the final arbiter on vital decisions; in exile, some of these same Cubans were prone to abdicate their judgment to the CIA, assuming that Washington knew best and that American support assured the success of any venture. In a sense, many exile leaders were seeking a colonial solution to a revolutionary problem. They accepted CIA proconsuls as political strategists and allowed themselves to be bullied by shadowy agents in Miami's hotel lobbies. As events were to show, this was not the attitude, nor were these the men, who could arouse much enthusiasm in Cuba, an island gripped by messianic nationalism.

II

Such was the background for the debate on sugar that occupied the first seven months of 1960. As we have described, the activities of the extremists in both camps provided ample leverage for driving Havana and Washington apart. It was a case of mote and beam. In Cuba, the continuing clandestine flights were the beam—and flirtation with the communist bloc was the mote. In Washington, it was the other way around. If Cuba were allowed to get away with its effronteries,—a frequently heard argument went,—a dangerous precedent would be set in the rest of Latin America. "The United States," exhorted George Sokolsky, who spoke for nationalist conservatives, "needs to take a stand against every speck of a country spitting in our face." Big powers respond to the same stimuli; the same words must have been echoed in the Kremlin when the Politburo took up the problem of rebellious Albania.

But what could be done? The most obvious club, lying right at hand, was the Cuban sugar quota. The more Americans studied the matter, the more intolerable it seemed that Cuba should cream off a premium price for its sugar. The assumption among many was that removal of Cuba's quota would cripple the island's economy and perhaps bring down Castro. There was an element of Marxism-in-reverse in this formulation—the concept that economic duress would affect political emotions in a direction more favorable to the United States. But all too often, economic sanctions can produce precisely the opposite result and solidify a rebel and his followers.

In any event, Washington was not thinking; it was re-acting. In a remarkably prescient column, Joseph Alsop warned of the consequences of becoming involved in an emotional orgy of tit-for-tat. Alsop wrote from Havana on March 14:

> Compared to Castro, Nasser is humble, sluggish and lethargic. If Nasser reacted violently to the beginning of a game of tit-for-tat, Castro can be expected to react ten times more violently. He can in fact be ex-pected to play out the game of tit-for-tat to the limit of his resources, without regard for the consequences to Cuba, or the consequences to himself, or any other practical consideration.

Cassandra was ignored, and inexorably Washington was drawn into games that only Castro could win. The games culminated in a violent exchange that involved not only sugar but also oil—of all products the most politically loaded and symbolic of imperialism.

As early as January 22, the late Styles Bridges, Senator from New Hampshire and influential chairman of the Re-publican Policy Committee, was calling for a review of the sugar quota in retaliation against Castro's seizures of American property. John Marshall Butler, Senator from Maryland, added a day later that the United States should re-examine its Cuba policy, "paying special attention to Teddy Roosevelt's maxim to speak softly and carry a big stick." If in the ensuing months Castro was able to caricature the American policy as Big Stickism, it ought to be noted that American utterances helped hand him this propaganda weapon.

By February, the Administration was sounding out Chair-man Harold Cooley of the House Agricultural Committee on changing the sugar law to give the President standby authority to alter its provisions. Cooley, on March 8, an-nounced that he had refused to sponsor the Administra-tion's measure because it contained "weapons of reprisal" against the Cuban people. More than compassion for the Cubans entered into Mr. Cooley's decision; he did not want to see control of the legislation pass out of his com-mittee, where he used his power for vote-trading purposes with legislators from sugar-producing states.

On March 15, President Eisenhower said, a bit disingenuously, that the request for standby power was in no way intended as an act of reprisal against Cuba but was instead a way of assuring that the United States would get the sugar it needed. But the stampede of events made it clear what the purposes of the request really were. Actually, the problem in sugar was not to assure supply but to limit it. A fecund crop, sugar is easily cultivated in either cane or beet form, and the purpose of the Sugar Act was to allocate production among many domestic and foreign growers.

In the succeeding weeks, the game of tit-for-tat intensified. The unrepentant Castro would kick and jeer; the lumbering giant tried to flick him away like a bothersome fly. On March 16, the Commerce Department revoked a license for the sale of helicopters to Cuba; the next day in Havana, Castro jibed back that he could buy helicopters from Russia anyway. On April 7, President Eisenhower released the text of a letter to Chilean students that first used the word "betrayal" in an official U.S. statement on the Cuban revolution. On April 20, the House of Representatives passed the foreign-aid bill with a rider tacked on barring any aid to Cuba unless the President should judge it in the national or hemispheric interest.

Then, in May, a swift series of calamities put the Administration on the defensive and made it all the more eager to take some action, somewhere, that could restore some American self-respect. On May 1, the fateful U-2 plane nosed into the skies over Russia and plummeted down, taking with it the hopes for the Paris summit and the plans for President Eisenhower's goodwill trip to Russia and Japan. At the same time, adding to the mad-hatter atmosphere of that memorable May, the Senate Internal Security Subcommittee on May 3 held a hearing starring one-time Batista army officers, thus providing an official forum for the most unsavory of all Castro opponents, as if to prove that Fidel was right in asserting that the United States was helping the Batistanos. The most notorious of the officers appearing before the subcommittee were General Francisco Tabernilla, former chief of staff, and Colonel Manuel Antonio Ugalde Carrillo, one-time commander of the military prison on the Isles of Pines, who was removed from that post by Batista after the prisoners went on strike against inhumane treatment.

The game intensified. On May 26, the White House announced that all existing aid programs to Cuba had been canceled; the programs were small—amounting to about

61

$150,000 to $200,000—but the step was symbolic. On June 3, a United States note accused Castro of conducting a "campaign of slander." Havana "categorically" rejected the note. On June 15, Cuba ordered two U. S. Embassy aides to leave the island because of contacts with counterrevolutionaries. On June 17, the United States retaliated by ejecting two Cuban diplomats. On June 22, Castro threatened to counter any action on sugar with total confiscation of American property. Four days later, the House of Agriculture Committee, under heavy pressure, approved a bill giving the President the power to fix the Cuban quota.

By cruel coincidence, this coincided with a crisis in Cuba concerning foreign-owned oil refineries. On May 23, United States and British oil companies in Cuba were ordered to refine Soviet crude oil, purchased to save the regime dollars and to forestall payment on some $60 million owed the oil companies for past deliveries. Immediately after the House Agriculture Committee's action on the sugar bill, Castro seized the Texaco plant in Santiago for refusal to refine Soviet oil. He said defiantly, "We will take and take until not even the nails of their shoes are left. . . . " By the end of June, Castro had seized the last two foreign-owned oil companies because of their refusal to refine Soviet oil.

In Congress, tumult prevailed. The legislators were impatient to recess for the political conventions and the President was reportedly furious at the prospect that there would be no final action on the sugar bill. Intense Administration pressure was applied as the two houses of Congress stayed in all-night session on the sugar bill. Emotions were frayed, and the political process was at its worst. Republicans and Democrats solemnly accused each other of being "soft" on Castro, and amid scenes of near pandemonium, the sugar bill was virtually written on the floor, in haste and in anger.

When it was over, the bill that emerged gave the President discretionary power to reallocate the Cuban sugar quota—but the law also made mandatory the provisions of a windfall bonus to Dictator Rafael Trujillo's Dominican Republic. Castro propagandists could have asked for little more; subsequently, the Administration had to return to Congress to obtain authority to deprive the Trujillo regime of its slice of the Cuban bonanza.

On July 5, President Eisenhower signed the sugar bill and immediately withdrew virtually all of the Cuban sugar quota for the balance of 1960. Then came a curious anticlimax.

Congress withdrew to the political wrangles of the nominating conventions and President Eisenhower departed for his vacation quarters in Newport, Rhode Island. There, he met with Secretary of State Herter to discuss the draft of a new hemisphere-aid plan to be presented at a forthcoming economic conference in Bogotá. Press Secretary James Hagerty said that the plan had no direct relation to the Cuban controversy and as yet had no name. Shortly thereafter, the Administration asked Congress, during its rump session in August, to authorize a $500,000,000 contribution to a hemisphere-development fund.

The timing and circumstance of the birth of what was to become the Act of Bogotá were ineffable. After years of delay, the United States seemed to take initiative on a massive aid program for Latin America only after relations with Cuba had plumbed the nadir. It did not help that the announcement came almost directly from the golf links ("The President," the Associated Press reported, "was in a jovial mood on the first full day of his vacation. He got 18 holes of golf after his arrival . . . and was on the golf course again by 9:30 this morning.") Cynical Latin Americans immediately dubbed the $500,000,-000 aid program the "Fidel Castro Plan," and responded with the remark "Gracias, Fidel."

While all this was going on, in the distant jungle of Africa a new country was born—the Congo—and a man named Patrice Lumumba was making headlines. The U-2 debacle, the crumbled summit in Paris, the riots in Japan, Cuba, and the Congo—that summer was not one to remember.

III

Indulging in the luxury of retrospective judgment, an observer can easily discern how a distracted and defensive country was led to strike back blindly at a taunting leader of a tiny nation. From today's vantage it is easier to see that the timing of Washington's moves was deplorable and the substance of its action questionable.

With a calmer country, the United States might have taken a different, more defensible, tack. Instead of suspending the quota, it could have set aside the premium payment of 2 cents over the world market price per pound of sugar, putting the money into an internationally administered fund. This fund could have been used to compensate expropriated land owners, with the understanding

63

that Cuba would regain the bonus when an honest attempt was made to meet legitimate American grievances. This would have meant that Cuba could have remained within the United States market. It would have averted the charge of economic warfare because Cuba would then be getting the same price for her sugar as other foreign producers not favored with the bonus arrangement.

Significantly, State Department officials were urging this approach, but the pressures were intense for a bludgeon method and President Eisenhower was too susceptible to the temptation to reach for a driver instead of a putter more suitable to avoiding the sand trap on a difficult tee.

The result of Washington's tantrum reflex was to fix in the minds of many Latin Americans the stereotype of a brave young rebel who was being punished for trying to exercise sovereignty and carry out a needed social reform. Latin Americans ruefully noted that there would have been no talk about "betrayal" if Castro had sold out his revolution to the United Fruit Company or the First National Bank of Boston.

Concerning the timing, Ralph Winnet summarized the case in an article in the *New Republic:*

> If we were secretly bent on glorifying Castro we could do it by adhering to a few simple rules: 1. Arrange the timing of all punitive measures so that they follow the confiscation of American property—especially oil property. 2. Proceed on the assumption that Latin Americans will naturally side with the United States. If this does not happen, evince hurt and surprise. 3. While United States owners are smarting from financial losses in Cuba, issue warnings against a Communist beachhead there. . . .

This formula was applied effectively to Mexico. On July 7, in the midst of the sugar fight, the spokesman for Mexico's dominant party in Congress, Emilio Sánchez Piedras, expressed sympathy for Cuba. The next day, the State Department summoned Mexico's Ambassador in Washington to explain what was meant by the speech. President Eisenhower himself was said to have called from Newport to ask about the matter.

According to Gerry Robichaud, the Chicago *Daily News* correspondent in Mexico City, there was "deep and lingering resentment" over the summoning of the Ambassador.

"Their attitude," Robichaud wrote, "is that the United States would be fit to be tied if foreign governments kept calling in United States ambassadors to explain the hostile remarks by United States Congressmen."

The incident, although trivial, suggests the pre-Castro attitude in Washington to Latin America. Not the least of the lessons administered by Castro to the United States is that a little tact and self-restraint, as well as pride, becomes the richest fellow on the block.

IV

Meanwhile, the Democrats and Republicans had nominated their presidential candidates—and in Miami, the Central Intelligence Agency was busy forming an army and recruiting a new government for Cuba. The details of the CIA operation will be set forth shortly; suffice it to say at this point that neither Vice President Nixon nor Senator Kennedy were wholly unaware of the CIA's efforts. Knowledge of this lends a revealing retrospective dimension to what both men said during the campaign.

In one respect, Mr. Nixon and Mr. Kennedy were evenly matched. Neither knew a great deal about Cuba or Latin America; both had to depend on the counsel of interested persons. Thus it is perhaps not surprising that the candidates were guided chiefly by the vicissitudes of the campaign, and less by inner conviction, in handling the Cuban nettle.

As regards Cuba, the campaign can be divided into two phases. The first phase, lasting until mid-October, was one of relative restraint and careful statement; in the second phase, the rivals reached for any available stick. Perhaps the best statement of their views in the initial phase came in a response to a questionnaire submitted by the Scripps-Howard chain. Question No. 4 was, "How would you meet the Cuban problem?" Mr. Nixon replied in part on September 23:

I believe the United States should continue to work within the framework of the Organization of American States regarding the Cuban problem, or any other which threatens the security of this hemisphere. We must recognize that there is no quick or easy solution to the threat raised by Castro in carrying out his extremist revolutionary policies and in his apparent desire to align Cuba with the Communist bloc....

In a nutshell, however, our policy toward Cuba

should be governed by two basic guidelines. For one thing, we should undertake to meet the problem in concert with our sister republics of Latin America. For another, we must put the world on notice that under no circumstances will we tolerate Communist intervention in the Western hemisphere.

We must realize that the use of force toward Cuba or any other sister republic is bound to reawaken Latin American fears of this nation as an aggressive colonial power. This would inevitably damage our own prestige and work to the advantage of the Communists and other anti-American forces in the Americas. . . .

There are grounds for hoping that if given the opportunity and the time, the people of Cuba will find their own way back to freedom and the democratic institutions which Castro has denied them. We must give them that opportunity.

To the same question, Mr. Kennedy replied:

I would have treated Cuba very differently during the last years of the Batista regime—when the serious errors of judgment and ommission were made. Our relationship to Cuba is only one aspect of the much larger problem of our relationship to all the nations of Latin America. . . .

If we can help create the conditions in Latin America under which freedom can flourish, then Castro and his government will soon be isolated from the rest of the Americas—and the desire of the Cuban people for freedom will ultimately bring Communist rule to an end. . . .

Meanwhile, we must use the full powers of the Organization of American States to prevent Castro from interfering with other Latin American governments, and to return freedom to Cuba. We must make clear our intention not to let the Soviet Union turn Cuba into its base in the Caribbean, and our intention to enforce the Monroe doctrine. . . . And we must let the Cuban people know that we are sympathetic with their legitimate economic aspirations, that we are aware of their love for freedom, and that we will not be content until democracy is returned to Cuba. The forces fighting for freedom in exile and in the mountains of Cuba should be sustained and assisted, and communism in other countries must be confined and not permitted to spread.

These considered words summed up the views both men espoused during September. But Democratic orators began to report that no issue drew as much emotional response as Cuba, and the Republicans began to press for some action that would signify that the United States was "doing" something about Castro.

At the same time, the Senate Internal Security Subcommittee released a report charging that Cuba "was handed to Castro and the Communists by a combination of Americans in the same way China was handed to the Communists." The report released on September 10 was based largely on the testimony of two disgruntled political appointees who had been ambassadors to Cuba, Earl E. T. Smith and Arthur Gardner. Despite its protests, the State Department was not allowed to rebut the testimony offered by the disgruntled amateur diplomats. To Democrats, still smarting from the charges by the Republicans that Mr. Truman had "lost" China, the temptation was too strong to rub in the parallel—if not in the crude words of the Senate Subcommittee then at least by innuendo.

Kennedy began hammering on the Cuban theme over and over again. In a major speech on October 6 in Cincinnati on Latin America, he blamed the Eisenhower Administration for allowing Cuba to become "communism's first Caribbean base." At the same moment he criticized the Administration for supporting the Batista dictatorship, Mr. Kennedy approvingly noted that ambassadors Gardner and Smith had warned "that communism was a moving force in the Castro leadership," but that the Administration had failed to heed their advice.

Mr. Nixon rose to the bait. In an October 18 address before the American Legion convention in Miami Beach, the Vice President said that "this Communist-Cuban regime" had become an "intolerable cancer" and that the time was now at hand "when patience is no longer a virtue." Added Mr. Nixon: "I say that our goal must be to quarantine the Castro regime. A number of steps can be taken to do this and are planned."

The next day, the Administration announced that it had imposed a sweeping embargo on United States trade with Cuba. The action was accurately interpreted as an election move to help out Nixon. Ambassador Bonsal was also recalled to Washington for consultation. The same day—

67

October 19—the Cuban delegation at the United Nations notified the General Assembly that Havana expected "a large-scale invasion" to be mounted in the next few days with the support of United States military forces. It was the first time that the Castro regime formally charged the United States military with taking part directly in hostile operations against Cuba.

In New York, Mr. Kennedy struck back, asserting that the embargo was "too little and too late" and that it followed an "incredible history of blunder, inaction, retreat and failure." "For six years before Castro came to power," the Senator said, "the Republicans did absolutely nothing to stop the rise of communism in Cuba. Our Ambassadors repeatedly warned the Republicans of mounting danger. But the warning was ignored. . . . " The Democratic candidate went on to urge more stringent sanctions and that the United States attempt "to strengthen the non-Batista Democratic forces in exile and in Cuba itself. . . ."

On October 22, in Allentown, Pennsylvania, Nixon accused Kennedy of advancing a "shockingly reckless" proposal that could set off World War III. He said that the "fantastic recommendation" for directly aiding the anti-Castro forces would, if not withdrawn, amount "to a direct invitation for the Soviet Union to intervene militarily on the side of Cuba."

The record should note that at this point Mr. Nixon was already giving his approval in private to the CIA operation in Mami.

V

The sharpest exposition of the second, frenetic phase of the Cuban debate came in the October 21 television encounter between the two rivals, the last of the four "Great Debates." This was the exchange that centered on islands —Quemoy, Matsu and Cuba.

Mr. Kennedy led off with his version of Cuban events, firing each sentence like a loaded howitzer shell:

> I look at Cuba, ninety miles off the coast of the United States. In 1957, I was in Havana. I talked to the American Ambassador there. He said he was the second most powerful man in Cuba and yet even though Ambassador Smith and Ambassador Gardner, both Republican Ambassadors, both warned of Castro, the Marxist influences around Castro, both of them

have testified in the last six weeks that in spite of their warnings to the American government, nothing was done.

Our security depends on Latin America. Can any American looking at the situation in Latin Amerca, feel contented with what's happening today, when a candidate for the presidency of Brazil feels it necessary to call, not on Washington during the campaign, but on Castro in Havana, in order to pick up the support of Castro supporters in Brazil?

Mr. Nixon replied in tones of earnest indignation:

Our policies are very different. I think that Senator Kennedy's policies and recommendations for the handling of the Castro regime are probably the most dangerously irresponsible recommendations that he's made during the course of the campaign. In effect, what Senator Kennedy recommends is that the United States government should give help to the exiles and to those within Cuba who support the Castro regime, provided they are anti-Batista.

Now let's see what this means. We have five treaties with Latin America, including the one setting up the Organization of American States in Bogotá in 1948, in which we've agreed not to intervene in the internal affairs of any other American country, and they as well have agreed to do likewise.

The Charter of the United Nations, its preamble, Article I and Article II, provide that there shall be no intervention by one nation in the internal affairs of another. Now I don't know what Senator Kennedy suggests when he says that we should help those who oppose the Castro regime both in Cuba and without. But I do know that if we were to follow that recommendation that we would lose all of our friends in Latin America, we would probably be condemned in the United Nations, and we would not accomplish our objective. I know something else. It would be an open invitation for Mr. Khrushchev to come in, to come into Latin America and to engage us in what would be a civil war and possibly even worse than that.

This is the major recommendation that he's made. Now what can we do? We can do what we did with Guatemala. There was a Communist dictator that we

69

inherited from the previous Administration. We quarantined Mr. Arbenz. The result was that the Guatemalan people themselves eventually rose up and they threw him out.

We are quarantining Mr. Castro today. We are quarantining him diplomatically by bringing back our Ambassador, economically by cutting off trade—and Senator Kennedy's suggestion that the trade we cut off is not significant is just 100 per cent wrong. We are cutting off the significant items that the Cuban regime needs in order to survive.

By cutting off trade, by cutting off our diplomatic relations, as we have, we will quarantine this regime so that the people of Cuba themselves will take care of Mr. Castro. But for us to do what Mr. Kennedy has suggested would bring results which I knew he would not want and certainly which the American people would not want.

In his spirited polemic manner, Mr. Kennedy had the last word:

Mr. Nixon shows himself misinformed. He surely must be aware that most of the equipment and arms and resources for Castro came from the United States, flowed out of Florida and other parts of the United States to Castro in the mountains. There isn't any doubt about that, number one.

Number two, I believe that if any economic sanctions against Latin America are going to be successful, they have to be multilateral, they have to include the other countries of Latin America. The very minute effect of the action which has taken place this week on Cuba's economy, I believe Castro can replace those markets very easily through Latin America, through Europe, and through Eastern Europe. If the United States had a stronger prestige and influence in Latin America, it could persuade, as Franklin Roosevelt did in 1940, the countries of Latin America to join in an economic quarantine of Cuba. That's the only way you can bring economic pressure on the Castro regime and also on the countries of Western Europe, Canada, Japan and the others.

Number three, Castro is only the beginning of our difficulties throughout Latin America. The big struggle will be to prevent the influence of Castro spreading to other countries—Mexico, Panama, Brazil, Bolivia, Colombia.

We're going to have to try to provide closer ties to associate ourselves with the great desire of these people for a better life if we're going to prevent Castro's influence from spreading throughout all Latin America. His influence is strong enough to prevent us from getting the other countries of Latin America to join with us in economic quarantine.

His influence is growing mostly because this Administration has ignored Latin America. You yourself said, Mr. Vice President, a month ago, that if we had provided the kind of economic aid five years ago that we are now providing, we might never have had Castro.

Why didn't we?

The words deserve to be quoted in full because they surely marked the campaign's low in political humbug. The arguments of both men were shot through with the kind of sugared simplicities that politicians feel the American people like to hear.

In Mr. Nixon's case, his outrage over Kennedy's suggestion on aiding Cuban refugees came with ill-grace from a politician who was privately supporting the same course. His use of Guatemala as an example of how to handle Castro undercut the force of his moralistic position on nonintervention. Not all of Mr. Nixon's listeners were wholly ignorant of the CIA's reputed role in the Guatemala coup.

As for Senator Kennedy, his argument seemed a curious blend of Chester Bowles and Senator Thomas J. Dodd, mentor of the Senate Internal Security Subcommittee. On the one hand, he condemned the Eisenhower Administration for its support of Batista—but on the other hand, he quoted, when it suited his purposes, the testimony of two ambassadors to Cuba who were the most notorious symbols of the pro-Batista leanings of the United States. Of Latin America, Mr. Kennedy spoke in accents of Bowlesian uplift, but regarding Cuba his essential policy was one that ultraconservatives could applaud.

George Sokolsky, a Nestor of the hard right, commented on October 31 that, concerning Cuba, Kennedy "has been on the right side throughout. He has been speaking in the voice of American history much closer to the spirit of Theodore Roosevelt than Franklin D. Roosevelt. He is closer to the nationalist attitude of the Republican Party than to the internationalism of the Eisenhower Administration. Certainly this country must carry a big stick or we shall become the laughing-stock of the Western world which watches little Cuba mock and twit the great United States that does not know what to do."

VI

Cuba, in the meantime, was acquiring new friends. On July 9, three days after Cuba's sugar quota was lopped off, Mr. Khrushchev spoke at a meeting of schoolteachers in Moscow. "We shall do everything to support Cuba in her struggle," Premier Khrushchev volunteered, adding that the Soviet Union had the rocket power capable of hitting the United States if the "Pentagon dare start an intervention." A few days later, the Soviet Premier went on to say that the Monroe Doctrine was dead. "The only thing left to do with the Monroe Doctrine," he jibed, "is to bury it, just as you bury anything dead, so it will not poison the air."

All this came on the eve of a foreign ministers' meeting in San José, Costa Rica, at which the United States tried vainly to get its neighbors to condemn Cuba by name. "What does it matter to us if the Organization of American States condemns us?" Castro asked on August 7, announcing at the same time plans to seize $913 million in United States property—virtually all remaining American investment in Cuba. His cockiness was enchanced by Soviet support (even though Mr. Khrushchev noted, on October 28, that his rocket threat was merely "symbolic").

On September 18, Castro returned to the United States to bait the eagle in its own nest. By this time, Castro had achieved one of his ambitions. He had become a world figure. He descended on the United Nations like a tribal chieftain arriving at a pow-wow of equals. There was swagger, style and limitless audacity in every move he made. If the competition of such rival chieftains as Nehru, Sukarno, Tito, Nkrumah and Nasser troubled him, he never showed it. Only Mr. Khrushchev, by banging his shoe and braying from his seat, managed to keep pace with Fidel.

The effect of all this on his American hosts was a process that Jean-Paul Sartre has termed "involution"—the process whereby civilized states fall victim of the same mores as their taunting, less civilized opponents. Castro came spoiling for trouble, like a cocky Jet invading another juvenile gang's sacred preserve. The State Department reported that it could not find a hotel to house the Cuban delegation, and great pressure was applied on a midtown establishment to accept the unwanted guests.

When Castro and his aides invaded the hotel, they had already made arrangements to move to Harlem. Inevitably, after an ill-mannered he's-a-bum, you're-a-bum exchange over a petty question of payment, Castro's marauders stalked out of the midtown hotel, leaving behind a litter of cigar butts, chicken feathers, uncooked steaks and towels profaned with shoeshine stains. Castro got the headlines he wanted when he packed his party into the Theresa Hotel in the heart of Harlem.

Speaking at the United Nations, Castro took a modest four and one half hours to present his case; some of his speech was spellbinding and eloquent, but his most memorable remark was that both Kennedy and Nixon "lack political brains"—an aside that earned him a reprimand from the chair. During his visit, he physically embraced Khrushchev, while his regime in Havana was completing the diplomatic embrace by recognizing Red China and North Korea. However, Premier Khrushchev remarked privately to Prime Minister Nehru that he felt Castro was a "romantic."

Castro's exit matched his entrance. His Cuban plane was seized at the airport by creditors, and the "Maximum Leader" had to fly home in a jet loaned by the Russians, leaving 31 Cubans stranded at the airport, luggage and all. It took a court order to release the official Cuban plane. Once back in Havana, Castro called Kennedy and Nixon "cowardly hypocrites" and joked that Mr. Khrushchev would get more votes than either if he stayed in America for six months. The Russian, he explained, was "a genial individual with great energy and a peppery disposition," while the American candidates were two "ignorant, beardless kids . . . puppets who are toys of the big interests."

The war of words had reached the point where a different kind of war seemed inevitable. By October 14, the entire sugar industry was nationalized and at the month's end there was little left to seize of any American property.

Again, the word "invasion" was heard. As November began, the Cubans were before the United Nations formally charging that a United States-backed invasion was imminent. The American delegate indignantly dismissed the charge as "monstrous distortions and downright falsehoods." Similar rejoinders met a series of other Cuban charges that a hostile buildup was supported by the CIA and the Pentagon.

On New Year's Day, 1961, the third anniversary of the
73

Cuban revolution, the Security Council was meeting to hear Cuban complaints about armed groups and mercenaries preparing to attack Cuba. A day later, Castro ordered all but eleven of 300 persons on the United States Embassy staff in Havana to leave their jobs or the island within 48 hours. On January 4, 1961, President Eisenhower broke diplomatic relations with Cuba.

Thus, as Kennedy was preparing to take over the presidency, Cuban-American relations had touched bottom. And the American people were about to hear strange rumors about what was going on in Miami, where busy CIA men were following Vice President Nixon's lead in treating Cuba as if it were another Guatemala.

CHAPTER FIVE

 ## OUR MEN IN MIAMI

Generals fight the last war and economists solve the last depression, the maxim instructs us. It might now be added that intelligence agencies conspire against yesterday's revolutions. In the case of the CIA, the Guatemala coup provided the model for the plans to eject Mr. Castro.

Indeed, what may be called a Guatemala complex dominated the thoughts of both adversaries for opposite reasons: to the CIA it was the promise that a facile, earlier success could be repeated in Cuba with relative ease; to Castro it was the mounting threat that a Guatemala-style operation would be set in motion against him. While CIA officials privately assured the Eisenhower, and then the Kennedy, administrations that Cuba *would* become another Guatemala, Castro began warning publicly as early as March 1960 that his country *would not* be a Guatemala. The wry aspect of this weird controversy over the proposed Guatemalization of Cuba was that the principal base for the CIA-Cuban rebel enterprise was precisely the territory of Guatemala.

From the outset, the CIA seems to have been beguiled by a false analogy. Because the agency succeeded in July 1954 in engineering the overthrow of Guatemala's President Jacobo Arbenz Guzmán, a Communist sympathizer, with the help of a ragged band of rebels gathered

74

across the border in Honduras and led by a former army colonel and basketball instructor of comfortably rightist political persuasion, it jumped to the conclusion that the same techniques could be used against Castro in Cuba.

Yet, to think of a Cuban operation in 1960 in terms of Guatemala in 1954 was as farfetched as invading Hitler-held Europe with the contingent used to silence the guns of Navarone. If this is an exaggeration of the difference in military problems, it is difficult to exaggerate the enormous political differences that the "black operators" apparently overlooked.

Guatemala under Arbenz was still a chaotic, hit-or-miss experiment in Marxist or communist revolution in Latin America. Arbenz, whose leadership qualities did not even remotely approach Castro's, never established the degree of control over his country that the Cuban "Maximum Leader" had gained by 1960. An energetic American ambassador, the late John Puerifoy, was at battle station in Guatemala, busily coordinating the rebellion from within. Unlike Castro, whose army and militia were being rapidly equipped by the Soviet bloc, Arbenz commanded ill-equipped, disorganized and not particularly loyal forces. Whereas Castro had some problems in controlling an anarchic-minded militia, he nevertheless enjoyed the advantages of insular isolation, while Guatemala had a largely unguarded frontier with Honduras. Finally and no less important, the Guatemalan experiment had not evoked the kind of political and emotional response throughout Latin America that was awakened by the Castro revolution.

The last point needs to be underlined, because even though the Arbenz regime scarcely electrified Latin America, the ill-concealed United States involvement in the Guatemalan rebellion had the effect of reviving the resentment over past Yankee intervention in the hemisphere. Latin America quickly became the arena for anti-United States demonstrations that the communists, otherwise still ineffective, were able to exploit. There was profound indignation among some of Washington's best friends, men like the respected Chilean middle-of-the-road leader Eduardo Frei Montalvo of the Social Christian Party, who led a protest march on the American embassy in Santiago.

The sour aftertaste was intensified when Colonel Carlos Castillo Armas, the new President and erstwhile CIA protégé, proffered Guatemala a blend of autocracy, corruption, scandals and general miasma. Some of the positive reforms of the Arbenz regime were quickly undone, and even the State Department was dismayed by the ineptness of the man whom the United States helped put in power to replace a burgeoning procommunist dictator.

When Vice-President Nixon visited Buenos Aires in May 1958—few had then heard of Castro—he busily defended the United States from the charges made by Argentine students that Washington was behind the Guatemalan affair. But the impact of Guatemala apparently failed to register on Mr. Nixon. In 1960, after trying for six years to assuage Latin American feelings about Guatemala, the Eisenhower Administration made plans for a duplication of the same undertaking on so vast a scale that concealment of United States complicity would be impossible.

II

A powerful case can be made for employing clandestine "dirty tricks" to eliminate the foci of communist infection in Latin America. Castro agents themselves carry suitcases of "dirty tricks" in seeking to export the revolution; the battle is not very "clean" on either side. But this is an argument that has not been settled at the Bay of Pigs and that will be elaborated in the conclusion.

But the corollary to accepting this argument must be the requirement that any such operations be conducted with a degree of sophistication. There must be an understanding of the nature of the adversary, his strengths and weaknesses, his ideological posture and his political style. Once the chinks have been detected, the proper wedges ought to be found to drive the leader and his followers apart. The tendency toward preconceptions must be averted and an over-all policy developed to meet the realities of the problem at hand. It goes without saying that a clandestine operation can be no better than the men who conceive and carry it out| In retrospect, one wishes that the British intelligence services had loaned political advisers to our men in Miami when they were trying to glue together an anti-Castro movement and were tripping over each other like hapless extras in an Alec Guiness film.

From the beginning, the CIA operatives took such a sanguine view of their ability to topple Castro that they were as much concerned with establishing the character of the successor regime. Thus, in a process in which one step led insensibly to another, the CIA wound up by virtue of its day-to-day decision—making powers as a kind of independ-

76

ent State Department operating not in embassies but in garish Miami hotel lobbies.

Taken together, the net result of a hundred separate decisions was to commit the United States to a counterrevolution acceptable even to those most anxious to restore the pre-Castro status quo. In Washington, CIA higher-ups denied that this was the coloration of the agency's operation, but in Miami it seemed that the CIA plenipotentiaries equated American interest with supporting the more conservative exiles who avoided talk about social revolution, land reform and other unpleasant topics.

In conformity with their preconception that Cuba was another Guatemala, the CIA operatives cast about for a potential Castillo Armas. They began subsidizing political organizations that they felt could be manipulated by the CIA. And as an inevitable consequence, the ubiquitous agents looked unkindly on other leaders and movements that failed to agree. Step by step, this led to an active undercutting of rival groups—ultimately this led to the failure to give effective support to a growing guerrilla and underground movement in Cuba. It also reflected an attitude of hostility to left-of-center exile groups by second-rate field operatives. This in turn affected the top level of the agency and resulted in a lack of understanding at the top. It is not clear to what extent the CIA attitude was ideologically motivated or was simply a response based on the agents' view of what was "practical" or "realistic."

III

The story begins in March 1960, when President Eisenhower first gave the CIA permission to organize the Cuban exiles into an armed force. Initially, there was no talk about a massive, one-shot invasion; instead the operation was reportedly sold in part as a contingency plan. The Cubans were available in Miami; they wanted to fight. Why not give them some training? Conditions in Cuba were uncertain, and anything could happen to Castro. Since no regular army forces existed in Cuba, it could be vitally helpful to have a well-trained, well-dsciplined cadre ready to move in.

In over-all command of the undertaking was Allen W. Dulles, the tweedy, pipe-smoking director of the CIA. Mr. Dulles had served in two world wars and under six presidents. During most of the Eisenhower Administration, his brother was Secretary of State, and his agency had become increasingly involved in handling political operations with only the slightest supervision. Mr. Dulles presided over the general outlines of the Cuban venture, but day-to-day responsibility was vested with Richard M. Bissell Jr., one of Dulles' three deputies. Bissell, a tall, dignified economist and one-time Marshall Plan official, was known for his scholarly discourse and for his success in developing the U-2 flights, an ingenious innovation that paid off handsomely until there was one flight too many. Both men had wide experience in intelligence work, but neither was ever deeply involved in Latin America—their backgrounds in intelligence and politics was mostly in Europe—and therefore neither had extended contact with the very special psychological conditions prevailing elsewhere in this hemisphere. And neither had ever commanded troops.

The actual handling of the Cuban problem in Washington was assigned to a retired army colonel in charge of the CIA's Latin American division, and then to his successor, also a former colonel, who had business experience in Latin America. It is not clear what the military command structure was in Washington and who actually bossed it.

The Miami manager for the project was a Central European (reportedly an Austrian) who had fought with French *Maquis* during World War II, who had contacts with the Office of Strategic Services and who then became an American citizen and an operative in the CIA, successor to the wartime OSS. He chose the cover name of Frank Bender, and this name was to become closely and publicly associated with the entire operation as it progressed from its strange inception to its tragic end.

This man Bender also had the disadvantage of knowing little about Cuba or Latin America, but those drawbacks, which included his inability to speak Spanish, were compensated by immense energy, monumental self-assurance and a commanding manner that succeeded in impressing a great many Cubans with whom he came in contact. He also had a curious habit of referring to himself in the third person singular when speaking to other people, with the result that his orders communicated directly to his Cuban associates included remarks like, "Bender wants this done or that done."

But perhaps the most important fact about Bender was his penchant for yes-men and his consequent favoritism toward those Cuban exiles who believed that there was nothing wrong in Cuba that a good counterrevolution wouldn't cure by turning the clock back. That Bender's orientation was at variance with those of two adminis-

78

trations under which he served was a circumstance that gave the entire project the peculiar political flavor that contributed to the disaster. His superiors in Washington gave Bender unusual discretionary power and took his word for much that went on during the months of the invasion's gestation.

In Cuba, the CIA worked mostly out of Havana and Guantanamo Naval Base. In Havana, the principal operative was well attuned to the realities of the Cuban revolution and the shifting nuances of sentiment that were so important to know in judging the reaction of the island if and when an attack came. Unlike many CIA "country chiefs" in Latin America, this agent had considerable insight into hemisphere politics, based on experience. But it is not clear that his views carried any appreciable weight with his superiors and colleagues.

With rare exceptions, the dramatis personae, both in Cuba and in Bender's ensemble, lacked any apparent background for evaluating what was happening on the island. One eminent exile leader tells of a conversation with a CIA operative in which the Cuban mentioned Victor Raúl Haya de la Torre, the Peruvian reformer who is as well known in Latin America as Hubert Humphrey is in the United States. "Oh," said our man in Miami brightly, "you mean the Brazilian labor leader."

It is a paradox that when the Soviet Union, Communist China and the satellite countries send agents and technicians to Latin America, the visitors invariably come speaking excellent Spanish and possessing a sound knowledge of Latin American affairs. Coming from the other side of the world, they possess training that was in melancholy shortage among American agents assigned to derail a revolution on an island only ninety miles from Florida.

This lack of background—springing partly from a general neglect of Latin America—accounted for part of the trouble. An added ingredient was the predisposition of many agents to measure reliability by the loudness with which a Cuban denounced Castro and communism. Thus in the eyes of key CIA operatives, former Batista officers were simply anticommunists who were more ardent about opposing the rascal who humiliated their army. This evaluation was swallowed uncritically by higher-ups in Washington. But to many Cubans the distinction between "good" and "bad" Batista officers did not exist.

The final point is mechanical. The CIA men were not only shaping, in effect, foreign policy, but were exempt from any meaningful outside checks on their activities. Indeed, they were in the enviable position of both organizing a clandestine operation and preparing the intelligence data through which the validity of the venture could be judged. A Secretary of State has to cope with Congress, the press and informed opinion; the CIA men worked in the dark, with the only check being the outraged protests of Cubans whose complaints were often dismissed as "exile talk."

IV

It was under these less than felicitous auspices that the intense planning for counter attack began. The political framework was provided by the signing of a "unity pact" among the main exile groups in Miami. This came about in the last days of May with the establishment of the Democratic Revolutionary Front *(Frente Revolucionario Democrático)*, which carefully excluded any persons connected with the Batista dictatorship.

At this time the exile community in Miami was predominantly composed of the first waves of refugees, who left because they were tied up with Batista, and a second wave that departed the first drastic reform measures taken by the Castro regime. In the circumstances, the five-man directorate of the Front was composed of probably the best men available at the time, although none had a name to conjure with in Castro's Cuba. This directorate conformed to the conception of what both the State Department and the CIA felt such an exile group should look like.

The five were Manuel Antonio de Varona, an honest, earnest, but unexciting former premier who had served in the government of President Carlos Prío Socarrás (the man Batista overthrew in 1952) and who was leader of the venerable *Autentico* Party; Captain Manuel Artime, the young chief of the exile section of the Movement of Revolutionary Recovery (MRR); Dr. Justo Carrillo Hernández, an able and highly esteemed leader of the anti-Batista "Montecristi" group, who had served as president of one of the government banks in the early days of the Castro revolution; Aureliano Sánchez Arango, a life-long revolutionary who had been foreign minister in one of Prío's cabinets; and José Ignacio Rasco, a courageous young man who had led the small Christian Democratic Party in Cuba.

Among the five, only Artime could claim an important connection with a significant underground group in Cuba—and even this distinction would not last long. Verona was the exiled leader of the small *Rescate* (Rescue) group

80

on the island. Sánchez Arango had a limited following among university students through his old Triple-A group. Carrillo's friends were intellectuals rather than activists. Rasco's faction was of little effective importance inside Cuba, although many of his people later distinguished themselves in underground work.

The "unity" of the front was a polite fiction; no sooner had the pact been signed than it was followed by the swirling dissension that typifies rootless exile politics. Glowering at the outer periphery were the well-connected and well-heeled Batistano groups, such as the organization of former Senator Rolando Masferrer, whose private army of "Tigers" had helped the Batista forces terrorize Oriente Province.

From the outset, an unhealthy dependence on the CIA characterized the Front. The agency operatives provided it with a headquarters building on Miami's Biscayne Boulevard, and another office in Coral Gables, paying the salaries of many of its officials and investing money in its newspapers and propaganda activities. Thus the Cuban leaders lost their independence of voice and action. This was the saddest aspect of the entire production: that many honorable Cuban exiles allowed themselves to become an appendage of a government agency.

By late spring, the military plans began to take form. The original idea was to create a compact striking force of about 500 who could be used as infiltrators, guerrillas, and even as a landing brigade.

The decision was made not to train any forces in the United States because the risks of discovery would give away the Guatemala-style pretense that no American help was involved. Early in June, the choice fell—appropriately— on Guatemala. Fortuitously, President Miguel Ydígoras Fuentes had broken relations with Cuba a few weeks earlier —and appositely, one reason for the break was that Cubans were accused of plotting an invasion of Guatemala. Rounding out the family affair, the name of Colonel Arbenz, who had just gone to live in Havana, figured prominently in the Guatemalan charges.

Ydígoras was sounded out as to whether he would allow the use of Guatemalan territory as a training base for the rebel force. "Tony" Varona, the Front's best-known leader, conferred twice with President Ydígoras. Agreement was swiftly achieved and Dr. Varona relayed to the CIA the news that Ydígoras was receptive.

Under the agreements, the United States was to provide

the funds, the equipment and the instructors for the rebels. It is not known whether any financial quid pro quo was also arranged, as in cases when a foreign government leases bases to the United States. But it is virtually certain that the United States made no commitment to Guatemala to aid in the transfer of the disputed colony of British Honduras (Belize) from Britain in exchange for the rebel bases. This deal was implied by President Ydígoras in a December 31, 1961, speech.

Although the Department of State is understandably reluctant to discuss the details, it can be assumed that its officials were aware of the furtive negotiations. On the working level, the arrangements were being handled by the CIA and its mysterious colonels. Soon the Cubans began jocularly referring to the "Cuban Invasion Authority," and the chances are that Castro's ubiquitous agents heard the joke and a good deal more about the preparations. By July 1960 Castro and Cuban propagandists were continually talking about an invasion being planned against their island. The United States denied it loudly, and indignantly.

With Guatemala as a firm ally in the secret undertaking, the physical preparations for the building of the rebel force proceeded apace. The mountainous Guatemalan department of Retalhuleu was chosen as the site of the first bases, and a wealthy coffee planter named Roberto Alejo made one of his ranges near the town of Retalhuleu available for the project. The Alejo family is close to President Ydígoras, and Carlos Alejo—Roberto's brother—was and is the Guatemalan Ambassador to the United States. Guatemala's Embassy in Washington soon became one of the clearing houses for invasion preparations. Members of the Embassy staff discussed the operation openly in letters exchanged with Cuban exiles in Miami. When Roberto Alejo came to Washington in the summer of 1961 to negotiate financial assistance for Guatemalan and Central American coffee growers, he pointedly reminded American officials that the first Cuban rebel base was on his *finca*. It helped him little, however, in the negotiations.

By late July, hand-picked workers watched closely by Guatemalan soldiers and CIA operatives began building an airstrip in Retalhuleu to serve the emerging rebel air force. The strip was needed for the aircraft to be used in flying supply missions for the Cuban underground since, in those days, the prevailing thinking was that an attack on Cuba would be in conjunction with the clandestine opposition on the island. The long-range strategy was to use rebel planes also for air support for commando groups that were to land in Cuba and contact the underground and guerrilla forces when the moment for a general uprising began.

The flying had to be done from Guatemala because of the risk of discovery in the United States. Additionally, the Federal Aviation Agency and the Immigration Service, working through the Border Patrol, had finally succeeded in preventing unauthorized flights from Florida. But there was a breakdown of coordination and the CIA and other Federal agencies frequently found themselves working at cross purposes. Thus federal agents interfered with splendid impartiality with the pro-Castro and anti-Castro agents.

In Retalhuleu, meanwhile, United States transport aircraft from the mainland and from the Caribbean Command in Panama began landing on the new strip, bringing military equipment, supplies, fuel, volunteers, and CIA instructors. Some of the planes carried USAF markings, others were unmarked. Camp facilities were presently erected. CIA and Democratic Front agents combed Florida for refugee pilots for the Cubana Airlines and the Cuban Air Force. As soon as a nucleus of rebel aviators was established, the CIA provided them with a number of obsolete World War II B-26 bombers and C-47 transports. The idea was to duplicate in Guatemala the models used by the Castro air force so that rebel aircraft, painted with the insignia of the Castro Revolutionary Air Force, could operate with more ease on their missions over Cuba. The B-26's were given to the rebels because Castro had inherited a group of the same planes from Batista. But one detail—the particular model of the B-26 in Castro's possession—was overlooked, and as we shall see, this led to the discovery of the whole aerial deceit.

The Cuban pilots were checked out by United States Air Force fliers from a jet fighter squadron. The Cubans were not given fighter aircraft because the distance involved in a round-trip to the island was too great to make them operational. Perhaps it could not have been helped, but the nascent rebel army was being equipped in Guatemala with lumbering and obsolete aircraft at a time when it was already known that Castro was importing Soviet MIG fighters and that Cuban air cadets were taking jet training in Czechoslovakia. Even without the MIGs, Castro was known to have three T-33 jet trainers which, as it developed, were enough to knock the rebel aviators out of the sky when the big fight came.

While Retalhuleu thus became the air center for the operation, six other training camps were successively established in Guatemala. One of the big camps was at the Helvetia ranch, not far from the air strip. Another was set up near a shrimp factory on the Pacific coast. Two smaller camps were placed in Northern Guatemala, dedicated mostly to guerrilla training. The most promising guerrilla leaders, some of them veterans of the Sierra Maestra campaign at Castro's side, were sent for advance training to the U. S. Army's Jungle Warfare School at Fort Gulick in the Panama Canal Zone.

Small camps and shipment centers were set up in the Florida swamps. One camp was established in Louisiana, where the swampy terrain was reminiscent of the Ciénaga de Zapata where the rebels were to land the following year.

V

The smooth progress of military organization, however, was not matched by political developments. The loudly proclaimed unity of the anti-Castro elements dissolved almost at the moment of its inception. The confusion was soon compounded by the appearance, in an already crowded arena, of new, important anti-Castro groups holding highly independent views.

The first schism occurred within the ranks of the Movement of Revolutionary Recovery and involved Captain Artime. Initially, the break concerned personality, but it soon became ideological as well. Less than a month after the "unity" Front was founded, Artime came into conflict with a faction within his own MRR led by Major Nino Díaz, and by Major Ricardo Lorié, a one-time Castro pilot. The two apparently resented the commanding manner of the smooth-talking young captain, and whispers began circulating that Artime was developing into a budding dictator. Artime, for his part, was annoyed that Díaz and Lorié—two of the founders of the MRR—disputed his leadership.

Whatever the precise causes, the split grew deeper. Miami's hothouse atmosphere of exile intrigue abetted the schism. Finally, one day in July, Lorié Díaz and several companions burst into the apartment of Pepita Riera, an anti-Castro radio announcer, breaking up a political meeting that was being held there and administering a sound thrashing to Artime. Thus, before they were ready to attack Castro, the rebels were investing increasing energy in battling each other.

The split within the MRR and the beating given Artime

84

weakened the captain's position as a member of the five-man Front directorate. A campaign began to oust him. But the CIA stepped in to protect its young favorite. By this time, it is probable that Bender and his colleagues had already settled on Artime as the putative Castillo Armas of the invasion army; CIA was not going to permit exile squabbling to upset its plans. This incident foreshadowed a trend which reached the incredible point, early in 1961, of the imprisonment of Artime's opponents and their ejection from the secret army.

Another political complication within the Democratic Front revolved around Sanchez Arango, a forceful and impatient personality who evolved from communism, in his youth, to a rightist orientation. In time, Sanchez Arango quit the Front and switched to another anti-Castro group in which he cooperated closely with Eusebio Mujal, who had been president of the Cuban Labor Confederation under Batista.

As airline flights from Havana daily disgorged new loads of refugees from Cuba, anti-Castro political movements began to proliferate at a dizzying rate. As summer gave way to fall, Miami began to take on the characteristics of a Cuban city, and it seemed as if every Cuban of any consequence started his own movement of liberation. Some were fly-by-night groups centered about an ambitious politician and his immediate family. Others were more substantial. One calculation asserted that there were more than fifty separate Cuban movements in Miami, merging and dividing like amoebas. Still other movements flourished among exile colonies in Puerto Rico, Caracas and Mexico City. In Florida, radio stations beaming programs to Cuba offered a nightly selection of speakers, each representing a different group.

It was not surprising that Castro's opponents within Cuba soon became disgusted with the political carnival in the comfortable haven of Miami. Presently, a powerful new underground movement came into being. Its emergence coincided with the entry into conspiratorial activities of Manuel (Manolo) Ray, a young American-trained engineer who had directed the sabotage section of Castro's "26th of July Movement" in Havana during the civil war and who later became Minister of Public Works in the revolutionary regime. Ray resigned from the cabinet in November 1959 when the moderates were being purged by the radicals. For nearly six months, Ray's friends in the new anti-Castro underground urged him to join in the nascent struggle against the regime. For six months, Ray resisted the blan-

85

dishments and concentrated on teaching architecture at Havana University.

Finally, in July, Ray decided that the revolution could no longer be saved and threw himself heart and soul into the conspiracy. Ray's own decision coincided with that of a large number of once devoted Castro supporters in the rebel army and in the government, including Felipe Pazos, "Ché" Guevara's predecessor as head of the National Bank, and Colonel Ramón Barquín, the military ruler of Havana during the first days of Castro's triumph.

The idea of men like Ray and his companions was to restore the revolution to its original goals of political democracy and social justice. They stood firmly for the continuation of the social reforms initiated by Castro. Many of the early MRR followers, displeased with the Artime facton, turned to Ray for leadership. The underground movement these new insurgents created was given the name of *Movimiento Revolucionario del Pueblo*—the MRP—or People's Revolutionary Movement.

Ray quickly became a major thorn in Castro's side. The MRP grew from day to day, established national, provincial and local underground chapters, collected money, dispensed propaganda and practiced as much sabotage as could be accomplished without help from abroad. It was an action, not a debating society, but nevertheless received scant help. Although explosives and weapons were already flowing to Artime's MRR through air drops and clandestine maritime landings, no material was made available to Ray's MRP. Whatever help Ray did receive came from MRR underground units that were more disposed to cooperate with the MRP in Cuba.

At about the same time Ray helped to found the MRP, independent guerrilla operations came into being in Las Villas and Camagüey provinces, and especially in the rugged Escambray Mountains, where the anti-Batista Revolucionary Directorate had conducted its "second front" against Batista. Plinio Prieto, a tough one-time anti-Batista fighter, Captain Sinesio Walsh, and Captain Oswaldo Ramirez, both veterans of Castro's rebel army, commanded the new guerrillas. Catholic student organizations in Santa Clara, the capital of Las Villas, established contact with the Escambray units and took upon themselves the recruitment of volunteers and the sending of supplies. An 18-year-old Santa Clara university student named Porfirio Ramírez, who was president of the provincial University Students Federation, led the student underground. Support even came from the city's high schools. Peasants in the Escambray area helped and protected the guerrillas just as the *guajiros* in Oriente Province had sheltered Castro from Batista forces three years before. William Morgan, the American veteran of the Escambray, who then operated a government frog farm, assigned his trucks to carry supplies to the rebels in the mountains. Ultimately, this gesture cost Morgan his life; young Porfirio Ramírez, too, was killed for his help to the rebels. The new anti-Castro movement was finding its heroes and martyrs.

VI

By early fall, 1960, the combination of the Escambray guerrillas and the MRP underground in the cities was creating a situation of open rebellion against Castro. The two movements were not linked, but in their own ways they became the most important anti-regime operations in Cuba.

Yet the CIA strategists in Miami had little patience with the underground. It was not sufficiently conscious of "security," they said, and it was too difficult to get trained communicators into the Escambray with radios. But behind these objections was the Agency's enormous reluctance to give a blank check to any group beyond its control.

The MRP was then little known in Miami, since Ray and his companions were not politically represented in Florida. But the Escambray guerrillas could not be wholly ignored. Stories about their defiance of Castro were circulating in the United States, and the Premier made no secret of his concern about their progress. By September, he had moved powerful militia units to the foothills of the Escambray, and had taken personal command of the operation. His own experience in the Sierra Maestra taught him the danger of tolerating guerrilla force. Peasants and their families were evacuated from the region so that they could not supply food to the guerrillas. Firing squads went back to work.

Nonetheless, by the first of the year Castro had still not beaten the Escambray fighters, despite their lack of food and weapons. Castro's personal physician, an Army major, was killed in a skirmish with the guerrillas, who controlled most of the big mountains.

This stubborn resistance had an impact on Miami, and with some reluctance the CIA drew up plans to help the Escambray insurgents. About October, Cuban rebel aircraft from Guatemala began flying occasional supply missions to the Escambray, dropping food, weapons and radio transmitters. But it was an unenthusiastic effort and the drops were too infrequent. Slowly, the pressure of the thousands of Castro militiamen began to yield results, and the perimeter held by the guerrillas gradually shrunk. The parachuted supplies started falling into the hands of the militia instead of the guerrillas. By mid-November, the back of the movement had been broken, and the guerrillas were fighting for physical survival. Anguished radio messages from weak transmitters desperately pleaded for help. But since the effectiveness of the guerrillas had diminished, the flights were curtailed, and a long agony in the Escambray continued until almost the eve of the Bay of Pigs invasion, which, ironically, entered the island only 80 miles from the former rebel stronghold.

The collapse of the Escambray resistance left the MRP as the principal anti-Castro movement within Cuba. Although the MRP was growing in importance, Ray realized that it could not go on forever without material help from the United States. The example of the Escambray was cruelly clear. Growing desperate, but also hoping that John F. Kennedy's election would bring an administration into power more disposed to work with the left-of-center MRP, Ray arranged to be smuggled into Miami in November 1960 to plead his case in person.

One of the authors saw Ray in Washington shortly after his arrival. Deceptively soft-spoken, Ray had the manner of a young instructor, and was given to understatement rather than the usual full-blown rhetoric of Cubans. His English was good, learned during his student days at the University of Utah. He was preoccupied but optimistic about the prospects for the underground.

He was asked about Major Huber Matos, the revolutionary hero who was jailed for "treason" for espousing anti-communist views. Ray said that the MRP looked to Matos as a symbol of what the movement stood for. He added, with a flicker of excitement, that a plan was underway to free Matos that day, but that nothing could be said about the details. A few days later, Ray was downcast by the news that the plan had failed; it had relied on collaboration with insiders at the Isle of Pines prison, but Castro apparently got a hint of the plot, transferred all prison personnel and mounted a heavy garrison on the island.

The argument that Ray presented to officials in Miami and Washington hinged on the political desirability of an indigenous revolt that would leave Castro without the final glory of martyrdom. He contended that anti-Castro activity had to be focused on attempts to wean away Castro's followers and encourage defection within the ranks of the rebel army. The United States could help the underground by supplying it with arms and equipment—but the MRP would refuse to submit to political domination by the CIA.

These conversations left no doubt that Ray was proud and in some ways a "difficult" person. He made no secret of his detestation of Mr. Bender, although his public remarks before and after the invasion were circumspect. At one point, after a phone call from the White House, Ray agreed to withdraw a letter he was sending to the New York *Times* outlining his difficulties with the CIA. It is an ironic footnote that CIA enmity cost Ray his leadership of the MRP after the invasion; the underground, feeling that it would never get any favorable consideration for help without a new face, asked Ray to step down.

With Ray's arrival in the United States, the two basic concepts of anti-Castro strategy collided directly. Ray wanted help for the underground tied in with a left-of-center political program; the CIA was in favor of an invasion presided over by an exile front with a cautious, moderate program.

At this point, however, the CIA was not wedded to a single, massive invasion. It talked in terms of multiple landings tied in with sabotage and insurrection within the island. As late as October 1960, Artime himself gave high priority to underground help. Discussing the operational blueprints with one of the authors, Artime spoke of a planned strategy involving thirty simultaneous air and sea landings by rebel forces designed to link up with thirty guerrilla and underground groups on the island. The quick-talking, chain-smoking Cuban explained that his rebels were already in possession of the necessary aircraft and landing ships to carry out the operation. Artime added that the exile forces were even forming paratroop units.

Artime is being held incommunicado in a Castro prison in Havana, and until he is free to speak it will be difficult to determine what led him to discard his own plans and accept the CIA proposal for a one-shot invasion.

VII

At the same moment that the Escambray guerrillas were collapsing in Cuba, the CIA army was reaching a high degree of preparedness in Guatemala—after a fashion. Recruits were being flown into the camps aboard unmarked United States aircraft from the deactivated Navy air-base at Opa-Locka, near Miami. Instructors were being assembled from a number of improbable places.

A United States Army colonel known as Davis was directing the conventional warfare training. A Filipino colonel who had fought against the procommunist Huk rebels in his country was flown in from Manila to work with the guerrilla and infiltration teams. Several Eastern European specialists, possibly anti-Soviet Ukrainians, whom the CIA had unearthed somewhere in Europe, were brought to Guatemala. Interpreters were provided to translate the instructions into Spanish, working with the training commanders.

But the entire operation was a study in military surrealism at least in the opinion of many Cubans who were there. Conventional solutions were proposed and executed for what was by definition an unconventional situation. Although it was obvious that a force of 1,500 to 2,000 men could not possibly defeat Castro in orthodox combat, the CIA planners built a miniature army on conventional lines. The Cubans were trained in World War II infantry tactics. They were provided with up-to-date weapons like bazookas, recoilless antitank guns and even a handful of medium tanks. It is difficult to imagine what kind of war the CIA was visualizing in Cuba, ignoring as it did that country's tradition of guerrilla wars going back to the Wars of Independence, as well as the political realities on the island and the staggering operational problems the little army would have to face.

The guerrilla training offered in Guatemala and at the jungle warfare school in Panama, such as it was, was equally inadequate, in the opinion of the Cuban fighters subjected to it. Most of the Cubans were veterans of the Sierra Maestra, and this gave them a certain authority in discussing the subject. Their opinion is that the Guatemalan camps they were trained on a terrain of granite volcanic outcroppings that bore no resemblance to conditions they knew to exist in Cuba. The tactics taught, therefore, were largely unsuited to the problems they would face at home. Several Cubans were sternly reprimanded by the CIA strategists when they suggested that the training follow more closely the instruction given the militia units in Cuba by Castro. In the end, a number of the Cuban guerrilla experts were expelled from the camps and returned to Miami.

By the end of 1960, the Guatemalan operation was nearing the periphery of public knowledge. Inquiring newspapermen were becoming suspicious about the strange doings at Retalhuleu and Helvetia. A Stanford University professor, hardly cast for derring-do journalism, found out about the camps and described them in a scholarly publication. But the Eisenhower Administration continued to profess total ignorance and the Guatemalan government insisted that the camps were for its own soldiers being trained in guerrilla warfare to resist an allegedly impending Cuban attack. When a group of American reporters were taken to visit Retalhuleu in January 1961, to try to bury the rumors about an exile army, Cuban rebel pilots were hidden in a shack away from the airstrip until the reporters left.

Although a good many perplexed Americans were inclined to discount the strange rumors about a rebel army, Fidel Castro followed the reports with the utmost concern. His network of agents in Central America and in Miami fed him the necessary details. He began a propaganda counteroffensive immediately, warning that an invasion was coming. Late in November, he ordered a general mobilization and charged that the Eisenhower Administration in its waning months would doubtless attempt an attack on Cuba. The militia remained under arms until Kennedy took office.

Havana and much of the Cuban coast soon bristled with fortifications. Gun emplacements dotted the curving seaside Malecón Boulevard in the capital, although it surely must have seemed unlikely to Castro that his enemies would wade into Havana Bay. But to further dramatize the peril, the Premier let it be known that strategic areas of the city were, or would be, protected by explosives and that he would blow up Havana if the enemy succeeded in overcoming its defenders.

It is probable that Castro was really convinced that an invasion would come about November. He kept hundreds of thousands of militiamen on the alert for nearly three months, although the mobilization took men from their jobs and the sugar harvest time was approaching. Hence Cuba's sinking productivity declined even further. Matters reached the point that Major Guevarra warned in a speech early in January 1961 that Cuba had to return the men to work to avert an economic collapse. Meanwhile, incredulous Americans dismissed the invasion scare as a propaganda stunt and editorial writers remarked that the new Administration would be too wise to fall into such an obvious trap.

The day of President Kennedy's inauguration, Castro ordered a demobilization. He remarked with satisfaction that the Cuban show of force had prevented the invasion, an argument that cannot wholly be dismissed. In addition, there is reason to believe that Castro hoped that Mr. Kennedy would seek an accommodation with revolutionary Cuba. He seemed to feel that the young President would radically alter Washington's policy toward Cuba. Consequently, Cuban propaganda was muted and Havana adopted an attitude of expectancy toward the new Administration.

But, on a political level, the new government had the same distaste for the Castro regime as did its predecessor. Operationally, as we shall see, it was caught in the growing momentum of the CIA's pet project.

VIII

A few days before President Kennedy's inauguration, the CIA moved to strengthen its hold over Guatemala—in effect, presenting his new Administration with a *fait accompli* in which the liberal elements among the Cuban exiles were swept from positions of influence.

This move, which the impotent Revolutionary Front had to accept tacitly, took the form of a *coup d'état* in the Guatemalan camps. On January 18, the rebel troops in the Guatemalan camps were summoned by the CIA agents in charge and informed that the new military leadership of the anti-Castro army was being placed in the hands of officers enjoying the special confidence of the United States. These officers, the assembled men were told, were Captain Artime, Captain José P. San Román and Captain Miguel Villafaña. Artime was the youthful member of the front, who had become the CIA favorite. San Román was a former officer in the Batista Maestra region. In the eyes of most anti-Batista Cubans, he was closely identified with the former dictatorship. Villafaña was the head of the exile air force, a strong-willed officer with a rightist reputation.

Other officers identified with the right-wing school of thought, including Batistanos, were given command of numerous units, including some five battalions of the rebel army. In Miami at the same time, the CIA and its Cuban associates arranged for the dismissal of the Front's "Chief of Staff," Colonel Martín Helena, a professional army officer who had resigned his regimental command in protest over Batista's 1952 *coup d'état*.

While the Front's leadership, except for Artime, was not consulted about the purge, the CIA came to rely extensively in its political activities on a shadowy group known around Miami as the "Cuban CIA," and built around the intelligence section of the Front. The head of this operation was Joaquín Sanjenís, a cousin of Major Sanjenís, the founder of the MRR.

The Sanjenís operation acquired considerable power in the opening months of 1961, when the invasion preparations reached the final stage. Working from its headquarters in a villa in Coral Gables, the intelligence group had the choice of which Cubans would be permitted to participate in the planning and execution of the assault on Cuba.

This power was reputedly used to eliminate from the preparations most of those who had cooperated with Castro in the early days of the revolution and who held reasonably progressive or liberal views. The foremost target was Manuel Ray's MRP, and during the months preceding the invasion this organization was deprived of any assistance, even though the MRP operated the most successful underground network in Cuba. While explosives, weapons and money flowed to Artime's MRR and to other groups that were not objectionable to the CIA's field operators, the MRP had to plead, bargain and fight for every pound of plastic explosives and for every submachinegun. Ray's agents obtained additional supplies by purchasing them on the black market and smuggling it into Cuba aboard their own boats.

Thus in the critical weeks preceding the invasion, the principal underground organization in Cuba was ignored by the very people who were planning the assault. At this time, the MRP was being described by its American and Cuban opponents as a dangerous movement advocating "Fidelismo without Fidel," whatever that was supposed to mean.

These wrong-headed activities went even further. Important groups of experienced guerrilla fighters were prevented from leaving for Guatemala even in the days preceding the invasion because those who directed the operation wished to have no fighters representing a different political approach. This was particularly and astonishingly true of a group of officers who had belonged to the garrison of Major Huber Matos in Camagüey and who had made their way to Florida after their commander was arrested and sentenced to prison for "treason" against Castro. Some of them, like their leader, Captain Napoleón Becquer, had escaped from prison to try to join the anti-Castro war. Guerrilla fighters who had escaped from the Escambray encirclement were similarly treated.

The exclusion of politically "unsound" fighters and favoritism for the pro-Batista groups continued even after President Kennedy has publicly assured that there would be no Batistanos among the Cuban freedom fighters. Similar assurances were made privately by CIA Director Allen Dulles, and it can be assumed that neither the President nor his intelligence chief had any idea of the meaning of what was going on in the secret little fiefdoms springing up in Miami and Guatemala. CIA higher-ups seemed to feel that officers who served in the Batista army were acceptable if they had a "clean" record.

Although a last-minute agreement between the Front and the MRP—forced on a reluctant CIA by the White House —called for the MRP's full participation in the approaching battle, the CIA operatives found ways of ignoring directives from above. A week before the invasion, the Becquer contingent and more than 100 MRP volunteers were ordered to go to Guatemala. But they were taken instead by the CIA and the Front's intelligence operatives to a farmhouse on the outskirts of Miami, near a spot called Bauer's Road, and kept there under guard. It is not known whether this action was taken with the consent or knowledge of Washington.

In the Guatemala camps, more than 200 troops who had objected to the January *coup d'état* were arrested on the spot. Most of them were released and shipped back to Miami, but a hard-core group—including several young lawyers—were kept in a series of improvised prisons in the Guatemalan province of Peten until after the invasion. According to their subsequent testimony, they were guarded by tough American CIA agents—imprisoned for the "insubordination" of refusing to serve under Batista military officers.

When word of these high-handed tactics reached Miami, at least one member of the Front—Justo Carrillo Hernández—rebelled against it. Although he refrained from making any public charges, he refused from that point to visit the Guatemalan camps. But his colleagues continued to make their periodic, morale-building inspection trips.

The CIA's position was that the insurgents who opposed the rightist leaders installed in the invasion army were unreliable and dangerous elements who had to be weeded out. It was implied that they were unreliable anticommunists, although many of them had been in Castro's prisons precisely because of their stand against the increasing communist inroads in Cuba.

Subsequently, the claim was made that the underground could not have been brought into the operation because the secrecy of the whole venture had to be protected. But those who advance this implausible case were oddly remiss in assuring this very secrecy in Miami. Although local police had a list of at least 100 known Castro agents, no serious effort was made by Federal authorities—who presumably were on speaking terms with the CIA—to weed *these* unreliable and dangerous elements out. As it was, the Miami operation was conducted with such astonishing indiscretion that Castro in Havana was as aware of what was happening as if he himself had sat in on the meetings in the bars and hotels along Biscayne Boulevard and Flagler Street.

IX

But even the pre-invasion purges were not enough, apparently, for the CIA operatives and their Cuban business and political friends. There was still one more arrangement in the dark to assure that a post-Castro regime contained no troublemakers.

. This top-secret project was known as "Operation Forty," and was set in motion in early March by Sanjenís and the intelligence branch of the Front.

Many details of "Operation Forty" are still shrouded, but enough is known to indicate that it was intended as a kind of "civilian-military government" that would move in on the heels of the invading army and take control of the national and local governments before the underground fighters could realize what was happening.

Curiously, the "liberators" were planning to repeat the policy of "Ché" Guevarra when he swept down into the plains of central Cuba and left his political indoctrinators behind in every town and village in his path. The difference is that Guevara planted procommunists, and the "Cuban CIA" was going to plant what at best can be called unreconstructed antirevolutionaries. As "Operation Forty" was being organized, it is worth remarking, the Kennedy Administration was eloquently affirming its support for a noncommunist but advanced social revolution in Cuba.

According to well-informed Cubans, "Operation Forty" also had a second task: that of assassinating, if necessary, political leaders who stood in the way. It was reported that the project included a hand-picked task force of professional killers who were to eliminate obdurate elements which might oppose a return to the good old days. In the confusion of battle, such killings could go unnoticed and the victims depicted as communists. One of the potential killers was reported to be Ramón Calviño, a Batista police torturer, a seaman who had been smuggled on shipboard and who subsequently went ashore with the invading forces and was captured by Castro's militia. In history's strange way, Calviño himself was executed.

The saddest aspect of all these blunders was that they obscured the character and motives of the vast majority of the Cubans who enlisted in the invasion forces. Only some 35 members of the invasion force were Batista soldiers who had bad records and the overwhelming majority of the rank and file were free of any connection whatsoever with the Batista regime.

They were brave, headstrong and democratic-minded young men who genuinely wished to restore freedom to Cuba. They were ready to risk their lives to eject a dictator and they entered the invasion force with the boundless enthusiasm of daredevil youth. Their gesture was gallant—whatever the other sad circumstances surrounding a venture over which they had pitifully little control.

CHAPTER SIX

 THE DISPOSAL PROBLEM

"The disposal problem." This was the crisp euphemism that Allen Welsh Dulles, director of the Central Intelligence Agency, used to describe an inherited problem on President Kennedy's desk. The time was shortly after Mr. Kennedy's inauguration, and the problem, basically, was what to do about some 1,500 men under arms, trained and equipped by the CIA, who were restively waiting for a chance to attack Fidel Castro's Cuba.

The outcome of the "disposed problem" developed into a classic instance of how a contingency plan can become an operational venture in the nether world of the secret service. When President Eisenhower first authorized the formation of the exile cadres in March 1960, no one contemplated a massive one-shot invasion. Instead, the small cadre was a contingency operation; ineluctably, the force grew—and so did the plan.

The wheel turned, a new President assumed office and

circumstances conspired to make a young Administration staffed with megabright intellectuals, the executors of an astonishingly inept scheme that on its own merits might never have been initiated. Not all the facts are yet known of the step-by-step process that turned the "disposal problem" into Operation Pluto. But it is possible to reconstruct something of the mood, the psychological flavor and temperamental combinations that played a vital part in resolving the "disposal problem."

First, there were the opposing personalities of Fidel Castro and John F. Kennedy, the young adversaries who were playing boldly for the highest stakes. Both had in common a background of family wealth, both attended respectable schools, both were fiercely ambitious, and both were men who could coolly estimate the odds and take a chance.

But Castro was a rebel and Kennedy was not. In whatever environment, Castro surely would have wound up with a sword in his hand as an avenging revolutionary. Fidel had little respect for the wisdom of his elders or the mysteries of traditional society. In contrast, Kennedy was a seeker of advice, a heeder of expert opinion. He came to the White House not as an innovator but as a specialist in effective political management. Whereas Castro cared little for the counsel of men of rank (especially if they wore a uniform), Kennedy at that time gave considerable weight to the words of the Establishment hierarchy.

Castro had already been in power for two years; Kennedy came into the White House as the youngest elected President, and he was palpably aching for greatness. After his narrow win over Mr. Nixon, the President was especially anxious to bring off a victory in the first months, to certify his title to office by popular acclaim.

Yet what did the President confront? At home, he faced a Congress with a reduced Democratic majority in which he was barely able to win a House Rules Committee fight intended to insure that his program would at least escape being stifled in the cloakroom. Abroad, the President encountered a no less disheartening array of problems—shapeless, irritatingly ambiguous, seemingly unbudgeable slagheaps of frustration. Laos was slowly slipping away, Berlin presented thwarting complexities, the Congo was a mess.

Then there was Cuba, so temptingly close to home. By virtue of his campaign speeches, the President was pledged to do something about Fidel Castro. An instrument was at hand in the form of the CIA plan—and, as we shall see, his respected senior advisers urged him to "let 'er rip."

But, along with many others, the President seriously underestimated his adversary. Fidel Castro may give the appearance of boisterous disarray, but on those questions vital to his survival he is seldom a "romantic." No simple phrase can sum up the personality of Fidel Castro; he presents an orchestration of dissonant themes.

There is the theme of genuine compassion—almost feminine tenderness—combined with crimson ruthlessness. There is his ambition to elevate himself—coupled with a need to bend his knees before a dogmatic political ideology. There is the theme of wanton destructiveness, evident from his boyhood days when he delighted in spraying the beach with bullets, and there is the theme of purposeful reform. But mingled with all of this is the motif of cunning. Notwithstanding his outward impetuosity, Castro has shown himself a gifted strategist in the tactics of entrapment. He does not meet his enemies frontally; he goads them on to self-destruction.

In fighting against Batista, Castro never exposed his handful of guerrillas to a frontal engagement with the army. He waited, he teased, and he finally conquered by forcing Batista to destroy himself. (It is not widely known that the total of actual *military* casualties during more than two years of civil war amounted to not much more than 350.)

The same stratagem was repeated when Castro took on the United States. Despite threatening oratory, Castro never provided the United States with a clear pretext for direct military attack—he kept his hands off Guantánamo Naval Base. He waited, he goaded, hoping to entrap the United States in a self-destructive act of folly. With the cooperation of the American government, and especially of the Central Intelligence Agency, he succeeded.

II

In no other country does an intelligence service operate with as much extravagant ballyhoo as in the United States. The MI-5 or the Deuxième Bureau, the British and French equivalents of CIA, are scarcely acknowledged to exist— and only cabinet insiders know the name of any officer except the director. But in America, the CIA has its headquarters right off a four-lane highway in Langley, Virginia, its existence advertised by disarmingly candid signs, "CIA— Next Right."

As with the plant, so with the personnel. The top men

in the Agency are listed in Government directories, and the director himself is given a place on official protocol lists. The organization's smaller fry—the CIA is said to employ about 30,000, a total higher than that of the State Department—seem to pop up at every Georgetown cocktail party, announcing mysteriously, "I work for the Government." Newspapermen have contacts at the Agency, and leading CIA operatives more than occasionally brief favored journalists with the inside dope.

In this sense, the "spooks" of the CIA have become thoroughly Americanized. Perhaps it is not surprising that in a country where celebrity is often a measure of prestige, even men whose names should be kept out of the newspapers feel tempted to puff up their own achievements. Allen Dulles, when he was director, was known to feel that his agency was not getting the public credit it deserved. Possibly this helps to explain why CIA sources themselves began quietly mentioning the Agency's victories, with the Guatemala operation appearing on every list. This tendency became especially marked after the U-2 debacle, which put the CIA on the defensive and made its officers anxious to justify its enormous budget, said to be up to $1 billion a year. And surely the CIA is the only "black" service that has distributed press releases about its personnel to incredulous reporters.

Thus there is a certain irony in one factor that led to the April 17 invasion: the CIA's increasing involvement in the news. Perhaps agents in the field took their cue from the men at the top; whatever the cause, CIA operatives in Florida and Guatemala seemed almost as conscious about projecting a favorable "image" of their effort as the United States Information Agency. Newspaper and magazine reporters were briefed by CIA agents, and Miami newspapers even took to submitting stories on the Agency's activities to the CIA for "clearance."

The fact is that it was impossible to keep the organizing of a small-scale army secret—especially if the recruiting was on American soil. By the time Mr. Dulles asked the new President what he wanted to do about "the disposal problem," the very publicity surrounding the operation made it impossible for the United States to extricate itself without a loss of face.

Assume that the President wanted to abandon the venture as a bad idea. This would have been taken as a vote of no confidence in the CIA, which had invested its prestige, money and personnel in a scheme that the organization adjudged sound. It would have been a blow to the Cubans who were supporting the invasion strategy, and who would be sure to say that the United States was a false friend and a paper tiger. It would have been gleefully hailed by Castro as proof that the United States had backed down.

These were some of the threads in the net of circumstance. Once the original order to organize an army had been issued, and once the army became the best-known "secret" force in the world, the avenue of strategic retreat was sealed off. Like a djinn released from the bottle, the CIA's creation soon seemed to develop a will of its own.

In their first meetings, Mr. Kennedy made it clear that he did not want to commit any American forces directly in the enterprise. What could be Cubans do by themselves? What was the CIA estimate of conditions within Cuba? Could the CIA present a plan for using the force in a way that would not directly involve United States military intervention?

Allen Dulles obliged, and the "disposal problem" shortly moved into another stage as a specific plan was submitted to the scrutiny of the White House, the Joint Chiefs of Staff and the National Security Council.

III

Meanwhile, "new hands" grasped the levers of state. Inevitably, this was a period of transitional uncertainty and organizational groping as the Government underwent a dislocating change of administration. Nowhere was this more apparent than in the sphere of Latin American policy.

The President came into office brimful of good intentions; his campaign had pledged an Alliance for Progress aimed at giving Latin America massive economic aid and encouraging social reform. During the Christmas season, the President's aides conferred in Puerto Rico with Governor Luis Muñoz Marín, and there was a mood of buoyant enthusiasm about the tasks ahead.

But a familiar problem recurred. The President had no one in his immediate entourage who knew anything about Latin America. During the campaign, his speeches on hemisphere policy had been handled mainly by Richard N. Goodwin, a bright, articulate, 29-year-old Harvard Law School product who had clerked for Justice Felix Frankfurter and who had worked on the House Oversight Subcommittee's exposé of Charles Van Doren before joining Senator Ken-

100

edy's staff. Pretty much by default, Goodwin became the President's chief adjutant on Latin American matters. But Goodwin, still new in the job and uncertain of his terrain, carried little personal authority in the discussions of the Cuban plan.

An "old hand" from New York came down to help out. Adolf A. Berle, Jr., was a veteran New Dealer who had served as FDR's Ambassador to Brazil and as Assistant Secretary of State for Inter-American Affairs. He joined the new Administration as the chief of a nebulous task force on Latin America that generated both new ideas and administrative confusion. A stout champion of a prodemocratic hemisphere policy, Mr. Berle was handicapped by his tendency to see current developments through the spectacles of the past. The 65-year-old braintruster was fond of using two analogies to explain United States policy toward Cuba. First, he would say, there were parallels with the immediate prewar period in Latin America, when extensive Axis penetration was abetted by Juan Perón. Then, by a show of firm authority, the United States forced Latin America to choose sides—and once again the United States had to do the same. He would also liken the hemisphere crisis with the postwar period in Europe. The action against Cuba, he would reason, is like the Truman Doctrine, a negative step to contain communism. Coupled with it was the Alliance for Progress, aimed at strengthening our democratic friends in the same fashion as the Marshall Plan.

Working with Berle on many aspects of hemisphere policy was Arthur M. Schlesinger, Jr., the Harvard historian who had joined the White House staff as a kind of troubleshooter. A shrewd veteran of intelligence service during World War II, Schlesinger brought a discreet skepticism to bear of discussions of the invasion proposal. But as a Harvard don new to the seat of power he was diffident about using his sharp tongue.

These three—Goodwin, Berle and Schlesinger—tended to fill the void in Latin American policy, a void partly caused by the Kennedy Administration's inability to recruit a suitable appointee for the job of Assistant Secretary of State for Inter-American Affairs. During the first months, an Eisenhower holdover, Thomas C. Mann, stayed on the job. Mann, a cautious career officer, was appointed at his own request as Ambassador to Mexico in early April. It was not until June, after more than twenty candidates had been considered, that the post was finally filled by Robert Forbes

Woodward, Jr., then Ambassador to Chile, ending the six-month search.

Hence the decision on the Cuban invasion was taken without the participation of a spokesman for hemisphere policy who might look ahead and consider the consequences he might have to cope with after the deed was done. This was another thread in the skein—the transitional confusion that made an orphan of Latin American policy.

For his part, Secretary of State Dean Rusk took a passive attitude toward the CIA adventure in policy-making, partly because his conception of his job was that of an implementer and not an originator of policy. Rusk actively discouraged subordinates from getting involved. A few weeks before the invasion, he placed in his drawer a memorandum prepared by then Under Secretary Chester Bowles, which expressed qualified doubts about the project.

Notwithstanding the confusion, the "new hands" were able to infuse new horsepower into over-all hemisphere policy. The Alliance for Progress became more than a campaign slogan. On March 13, the President spoke at a White House reception for Latin American diplomats and called for a vast Ten-Year-Plan to transform the 1960's into "an historic decade of democratic progress." After years of dilatory indifference, the United States had finally ended its *mañana* attitude toward Latin America and had begun talking in terms of a Marshall Plan for a region that needed nothing less.

But the President's ambivalence toward Cuba was also still apparent. On February 9, it became known that Earl E. T. Smith, the one-time Ambassador to Batista's Cuba and a next-door neighbor in Palm Beach to Joseph P. Kennedy, had been nominated as Ambassador to Switzerland. The announcement startled democratic-minded Cubans, and it troubled the Swiss government, which had undertaken to represent United States interests in Cuba following the diplomatic break between Havana and Washington. Adverse comment from Switzerland led Mr. Smith to withdraw his name. On February 22, President Kennedy accepted Smith's decision with "real regret."

IV

The "disposal problem," in the meantime, was being hastily processed in the mills of bureaucracy. Allen Dulles and his aide, Richard Bissell, submitted the outline of a plan calling for an invasion by exile forces after a bombing raid had knocked out Castro's air power on the ground.

In March, the President called the first of a series of meetings that took place over a ten-week period and that dealt with the Cuban plan. Among those who attended the various sessions, besides the CIA spokesman, were Secretary of State Rusk; Secretary of Defense Robert McNamara; General Lyman Lemnitzer, chairman of the Joint Chiefs of Staff; Admiral Arleigh Burke, Chief of Naval Operations; Adolf A. Berle, Jr., head of the Latin American task force; and McGeorge Bundy, the President's special assistant for national security affairs.

The attitude of the CIA officials at the discussion was one of enthusiastic partisanship. "Allen and Dick didn't just brief us on the Cuban operation," a White House adviser told Stewart Alsop, "they sold us on it." Subsequent to the invasion, the story went around immediately that the CIA never expected Castro to fall at once and that at best their hope was to establish a beachhead, achieving a partial victory. This view was stated publicly for the first time by Allen Dulles when he appeared on "Meet the Press" on December 31, 1961, shortly after his retirement. John Steele of *Time* magazine asked Dulles "very frankly whether the failure in Cuba was an intelligence failure." Dulles replied: "I do not think it was, Mr. Steele. There was no military hardware that appeared that was a surprise to us. Some of the material was handled a little better than we expected. There is a quite general popular misapprehension that it was felt that there would be a spontaneous uprising. We had never contemplated that. The days of the war I worked a great deal with the French underground. The last thing we wanted was spontaneous uprisings to get slaughtered by the Nazi troops. In the same way we were not looking for a spontaneous uprising, but for other developments."

However, those who were involved in the discussions in March tell quite a different story; they assert that no such limited-victory impression was left by Mr. Dulles. Whatever qualifications he may have offered at the time were lost in his rosy prediction that after a beachhead was secured, large-scale defections could be expected within days.

Among the arguments advanced by the CIA in favor of the plan was the assertion that it was now or never—an estimate that Mr. Dulles reiterated publicly in his "Meet the Press" interview. It was known that Castro had Soviet MIG fighters in crates and that Cuban fliers were training in Czechoslovakia. This meant that Castro would soon be unbeatable by any outside force that relied on conventional prop-driven aircraft. Moreover, the Cuban exile forces were set to go; further delays would wreck morale. And Guatemala's President, Miguel Ydígoras Fuentes, was pressing for a solution of "the disposal problem" because the camps in his country had become a difficult political issue. While Ydígoras set no specific deadline, June 1 was spoken of as the date by which the camps would have to be cleared out.

Throughout, the CIA's double role as an intelligence gathering and policy-making instrument hampered an objective appraisal of the assumptions on which the venture rested. In effect, the Agency was saying that its plan was sound and that it was backed up by its own intelligence estimates. There is no evidence that the CIA availed itself of an independent check of its estimates, either by consulting foreign sources or other available American data. Indeed, those close to the operation say that the CIA did not even consult its own intelligence estimates of anti-Castro sentiment within Cuba—estimates that were reportedly more pessimistic than those offered by enthusiastic Cuban exiles in Miami.

"They fell in love with the plan and ceased to think critically of it," one official recalls. A CIA colleague of Bissell's added another point. "During these weeks Dick was overworking himself. He was at the office twelve and fourteen hours a day. I'm sure he thought he was serving his country, but he might have served it better by leading a more normal schedule, reading the newspapers, and keeping in contact with common-sense reality. As it was, he was isolated in a kind of weird world of secret reports day and night."

Swayed by the CIA partisanship, the military went along. For some time, Pentagon officials felt restive and frustrated about the Eisenhower policy of "restraint and forebearance." As early as 1958, when Raúl Castro's guerrilla forces kidnapped Navy personnel and other Americans working near Guantánamo, Admiral Burke had reportedly urged direct military reprisals against the rebels. Burke became a frequent orator on the evils of Castroism, and there is reason to believe that nothing would have suited the Admiral more than a chance to show what the Marines could do.

The plan orginally prepared during the Eisenhower Administration provided for a greater degree of direct United States participation, in the form of more direct American participation in the air operation. Such American involvement was dropped with the full acquiescence of the CIA

104

and the Pentagon, when Kennedy said that the Cubans should be on their own. Other modifications were also approved—there would be no flights from American soil, no planes except obsolete models, and no fighter escort of the preliminary bombing raid because the distance from Cuba to Guatemala was too great.

Subsequent stories, most notably an article in *Fortune* by Charles J. V. Murphy, have sought to exonerate the Joint Chiefs on the grounds that these original concessions weakened the plan and that the subsequent cancellation of a "second strike," along with a few last-minute changes in details, doomed the enterprise altogether. But the Joint Chiefs went along with the preliminary modifications when they might have pointed out that the very ground rules meant that the success of the entire plan would hang by a slender thread.

Some have speculated that there may have been doubts about the military soundness of the plan, but that Pentagon officials expected the President to flash the go-ahead for direct United States intervention should the invasion founder; others assert that this gives the Joint Chiefs too much credit for Machiavellian ingenuity. In any event, the CIA received the stamp of approval at the highest level by men who were supposed to be granite-headed realists— and that approval, let us repeat again, was within the framework of the President's decision that whatever was done should be without direct United States military participation.

V

While Washington debated grand strategy, Cuban exiles were concerned about what the new Administration was going to do about the confused situation in Miami. The more conservative groups were apprehensive; their close working relationship with CIA agents seemed in jeopardy as Mr. Kennedy took over. The left-of-center groups were frankly exultant. They were persuaded that the days of CIA favoritism in Miami to the right-wing were over.

Their hopes were largely in vain. During February, the exiles, and some interested American citizens, repeatedly warned Administration officials of the presence of Batistanos in the training camps. At one point, in early March, these sources reported in dismay that a recruiting office for the camps had opened in Miami staffed with Batistanos. Felix Gutiérrez, once an officer in Batista's military intelligence

SIM, was in charge, and a zealous but ignorant CIA agent reportedly sat at his side. Among those registered for service in the office was former Senator Rolando Masferrer, the most notorious of the Batista henchmen in Florida. It took a week to remedy the blunder. At the same time, Liberal-minded exiles complained that Radio Swan, the CIA-financed station, was beaming broadcasts to Cuba charging that Manolo Ray and the MRP were "crypto-communists."

One reason for the confusion over the extent of Batistano participation was a sematic problem. Top CIA men frankly did not regard as Batistanos those professional soldiers who were majors and colonels in the Batista army but otherwise had clean records. This distinction simply did not exist in Cuba, where any officer who wore a Batista uniform was assumed guilty as a "war criminal" until proven innocent.

By March, MRP representatives who passed through Washington were wholly disheartened. Their disillusionment touched bottom when, on March 18, in a hotel lobby in Miami, unity negotiations with the *Frente* were conducted in the presence of a CIA man. During the meeting, a list of eighteen names was produced, and the Cubans were told that ten of the names had to be included in any coalition front. Among the eighteen listed were Julio Lobo, the Cuban sugar king; Dr. Carlos Márquez Sterling, who was known as "Ambassador Smith's candidate" in the bayonet backed elections held by Batista in November, 1958; and Agustín Batista, no relative to the dictator but one of the wealthiest financiers in the pre-Castro era.

On March 19, the confusion and distemper had reached the point that the MRP met in Miami to discuss disbanding the organization. "We can't fight Castro and the CIA at the same time," a bitter MRP spokesman remarked to one of the authors. But, as the MRP was meeting, a major turnabout in United States policy seemed to occur. White House aides, irritated by CIA favoritism to the right in Miami, of which they had finally become aware, sent down an ultimatum: either the left-of-center MRP would be included in the coalition or the whole venture would be dropped.

On March 20, astonished MRP leaders were offered the very terms that had been rejected in unity negotiations the week before. The central points were solemnly agreed upon: (1) any military operations would be under Cuban control; (2) priority would be given to helping the underground in Cuba; and (3) all Batistanos would be removed from the training camps.

As it developed, none of the conditions worked out at the unity meeting were honored. Moreover, MRP leaders were told that the unpopular Mr. Bender had been assigned to other duties; later, they learned that the ubiquitous Mr. B. had simply changed locale but was still very much in command of the Miami operation.

Events moved swiftly. On March 22, agreement was reached on a "provisional government" under the leadership of Dr. José Miró Cardona, with the Front's "Tony" Varona and the MRP's Manolo Ray as his chief lieutenants. Dr. Miró Cardona, a respected moderate, had served as Fidel Castro's first premier. In his new role he tried to serve as an honest broker, but like other men caught in the middle, the warm and affectionate Cuban was unable to do more than preside over a conflict between basically opposing attitudes.

The new coalition was obviously a shotgun marriage. The MRP still held to its view that an internal solution, relying on the underground, was the sound approach, and that the appeal of the new rebels had to be based on a genuine acceptance of the revolution's usable legacy of social reform. But the Front was oriented toward an invasion and advanced an essentially cautious social program. The Revolutionary Council suffered from the incurable defect of being an artificial creation which threw together representatives of the new generation and aging stalwarts of the old democratic movement in Cuba who were honorable but ineffective men.

At a March 22 press conference at the Biltmore Hotel in New York City, the birth of the Revolutionary Council was announced. Dr. Miró Cardona said that the Council would become the provisional government of Cuba as soon as its forces had secured "a piece of Cuban soil." Shortly afterwards, the Council released its "minimum program"— with an assist from Adolf Berle, who, ironically, had to caution the Cubans against placing excessive stress on the restoration of American property seized by Castro.

The program was an effort to paper over basic differences. The Council pledged a return to the model Cuban Constitution of 1940 and endorsed land reform, but its pledges on private enterprise seemed to be addressed more to an American than a Cuban audience. "We emphatically assure those who have been unjustly dispossessed," the Council declared in its declaration of war against Castro, "that all their assets shall be returned."

At the same time, it was specifically noted that the MRP maintained a separate position on two points: (1) that those foreign-owned utilities—power, telephones, transportation, etc.—that had been nationalized would remain state enterprises with fairer compensation to previous owners; and (2) that foreign banks would remain under national direction.

With this "jerry-built" structure finally assembled, the Cubans were ready to mobilize. At this point, a misunderstanding occurred that was to persist for months. Evidently, Dr. Miró Cardona and Tony Varona were under the impression that the United States was prepared to backstop the entire operation. On April 7, Dr. Miró Cardona came to Washington and conferred with Adolf Berle, who attempted to make clear that the Cubans were on their own. On April 14, three days before the invasion, Berle and Schlesinger flew to New York and saw Miró Cardona again, informing him that the President meant what he said in asserting that no United States forces would be involved.

The Cubans apparently heard the assurances with only one ear—and did not inform their countrymen in the invasion force, who subsequently protested that the United States had let them down. It is possible that the Cuban leaders simply could not believe that Washington could stand by and watch the venture fail after investing so much prestige in the plan. Perhaps the Cubans were acting on a reflex born of their experience in living on an island where the United States traditionally had the final say. This might explain why the Council's leaders accepted CIA direction so passively; the more the United States took over the management of the invasion, the less the chance the venture would fail. The shadow of the Platt Amendment hung over the frenetic deliberations between Cuba and the United States.

VI

As the "disposal problem" came near resolution, the United States found itself caught in a net of contradictions and confusions arising from a situation with no parallel in American history.

There was the ideological muddle caused by the difference in approach between the White House and the CIA political strategists. On April 3, the State Department released a White Paper on Cuba, a brilliantly written document from the pen of Arthur M. Schlesinger, Jr. It began with indictment of the Batista regime:

The character of the Batista regime in Cuba made

a violent popular reaction almost inevitable. The rapacity of the leadership, the corruption of the government, the brutality of the police, the regime's indifference to the needs of the people for education, medical care, housing, for social justice and economic opportunity—all these, in Cuba as elsewhere, constituted an open invitation to revolution.

The White Paper went on to outline in detail how Castro had promised a democratic revolution and delivered a totalitarian regime. It gave chapter and verse on the relentless communist advance, and concluded with this exhortation:

The people of Cuba remain our brothers. We acknowledge past omissions and errors in our relationship to them. The United States, along with other nations of the hemisphere, expresses a profound determination to assure future democratic governments in Cuba full and positive support in their effort to help the Cuban people achieve freedom, democracy and social justice. . . .

Because the Castro regime has become the spearhead of attack on the inter-American system, that regime represents a fateful challenge to the inter-American system. For freedom is the common destiny of our hemisphere— freedom *from* domestic tyranny and foreign intervention, *from* hunger and poverty and illiteracy, freedom *for* each person and nation in the Americas to realize the high potentialities of life in the twentieth century. [Emphasis in the original]

Hailed at the time by liberal-minded Cubans, the White Paper was made to sound like a cynical joke when Castro was all to prove extensive Batistano participation in the Cuban invasion.

A second dilemma was posed by the legal ambiguity of the CIA operation in Florida, which ran counter to international treaties and national law. Department of Justice and FBI officials were often unaware what another agency of the United States Government was doing. It became impossible to enforce the law without running the risk of one Government agency handcuffing henchmen of another Government agency.

The dilemma was uncomfortably posed by the indictment, early in April, of Rolando Masferrer on grounds of violating the Neutrality Act. The political purpose of the indictment was to demonstrate that the United States was not working with the Batista exiles, of whom Masferrer was the most notorious. The statute under which Masferrer was indicted (U.S. Code, Title 18, Section 960) is aimed at a suspect who "knowingly begins . . . or provides or prepares a means for" a military expedition against a country with which the United States is at peace. At a Justice Department press conference, a reporter asked if Dr. Miró Cardona could not be indicted under the same law. There was no comment. Others needlingly pointed out that Allen Dulles could also be booked on the same charges.

A related problem concerned Ambassador Adlai Stevenson at the United Nations. Stevenson had been informed, but not consulted, on the CIA plan. The President expressed concern several times that whatever was done, Stevenson was to be protected and not placed in the position of having his prestige at the U.N. impaired. The President's apprehension was real, but in the confusion his fear was to be realized.

All these and other problems were in the air when the President called an April 4 meeting of the National Security Council in order to have a full-dress debate on the plan. The meeting took place in a conference room in the new wing of the State Department. Those attending included Allen Dulles, Richard Bissell, General Lemnitzer, Secretary of State Rusk, Secretary of Defense Robert McNamara, Adolf Berle, Arthur M. Schlesinger Jr., McGeorge Bundy, Assistant Secretary of State Thomas Mann, Assistant Secretary of Defense Paul Nitze, Secretary of the Treasury Douglas Dillon, and Senator J. William Fullbright, Chairman of the Senate Foreign Relations Committee.

After Dulles and Bissell outlined the plan, the President pointed his finger around the room, inviting opinions. All members of the official family who were asked supported the plan, including Secretary of State Rusk. According to Stewart Alsop, whose version of the meeting has been authenticated as essentially accurate, one adviser said "Let 'er rip." Schlesinger, who opposed the plan on the ground that it would not work, was not asked to comment; he did not volunteer his views, feeling reluctant as a new man in town to pit his expertise against the Joint Chiefs and CIA.

The one dissenting voice at the pivotal meeting was that of Senator Fulbright.

VII

If any figure emerges with honor during those distraught days, it is the junior Senator from Arkansas. Characteristically, Senator Fulbright has refused to make any capital whatever out of his opposition to the invasion. He has been embarrassed by those who praise his prescience. The Senator declined to see the authors for an interview to discuss his part in the decision.

In December, Fulbright had been among the candidates Mr. Kennedy was considering for Secretary of State. But objections were strong, especially from liberal groups critical of Fulbright's opposition to civil-rights legislation.

The Senator's position on the Cuban controversy was outlined in a detailed, single-spaced memorandum which he submitted to the President on March 29. According to those familiar with Fulbright's views, his memorandum followed these lines:

Two courses, the Senator felt, were open to the United States in dealing with Cuba. The choice was between a policy aimed at overthrow of the Castro regime or one of toleration combined with efforts to isolate Castroism.

Concerning overthrow, unaided internal forces are not strong enough to do this job. But the problem posed by an outside attack, the Senator contended, is that it would be impossible to conceal the United States' role. The long-range damage, therefore, would probably outweigh any short-term gain in getting rid of Castro.

Furthermore, the Senator doubted that the exile groups favored by the United States as a successor government to Castro possessed effective leadership. The result would be that the United States would be blamed for the failings of a post-Castro regime.

If the invasion should fail, Senator Fulbright cautioned, the United States could be driven to direct intervention of a kind that would undo the work of thirty years in developing a Good Neighbor policy.

The Senator felt that the venture would be a violation of the spirit and possibly the letter of United States laws, as well as treaties which this country had signed. This point would be damaging in the United Nations and would not rest easily on the American conscience.

As an alternative approach, the Senator suggested a policy of toleration based on the premise that the Castro regime was a thorn in the flesh but not a dagger at the heart. While Castro offers a worrisome base for communist penetration, the long-range prospects are that by virtue of his extravagances he will isolate himself in the hemisphere and will be vulnerable to internal opposition.

The United States, Fulbright held, should place its emphasis on the Alliance for Progress as a means of isolating Castro and providing a competitive attraction to the Cuban revolution.

These were Fulbright's major contentions. What is striking about his case is that it is precisely the argument that one would expect the Secretary of State to make in behalf of a Department that must consider the manifold implications of a gamble like the invasion. But the case was made by the chairman of the Senate Foreign Relations Committee, outside the official family.

At the April 4 meeting, Senator Fulbright reiterated his position with force and eloquence. Some who were present felt that the Arkansas Senator had carried the day. The President, they say, was visibly impressed by Fulbright's statement. But Mr. Kennedy did not disclose his own views. He retired to the White House to give "the disposal problem" a final night's thought.

VIII

That April night, as President Kennedy mulled over a cruel decision, he was in a markedly different position from that of any of his advisers. He had to view the Cuban venture not as a game in itself, but as a single chesspiece on a constantly shifting board. Remember that at that time the United States also confronted the possiblity that American troops might have to be committed to distant Laos. What would have pleased Mr. Khrushchev more than seeing the United States mired in two exasperating limited wars at the same time? Moreover, if the United States acted directly against Cuba, the result would surely be to cloud Washington's claim of aggression against the communist bloc in Laos. Those who say that Mr. Kennedy assured the failure of the Cuban venture for mere "political" reasons tend to overlook the anguishing choices that faced the President.

Ironically, in the case of both Laos and Cuba, the CIA was blamed for similar independent machinations that compromised the United States. In Laos, too, the CIA reportedly had shown a predilection for the right and a tendency to decide for itself what the foreign policy of the United States should be.

Regarding Cuba, this was the dubious legacy Mr. Kennedy inherited:

1. A costly investment in an exile army of about 1,500 men who were insistently demanding a chance to show

what they could do. To disband the operation would be to dishonor an implicit commitment made during the Eisenhower years.

2. A policy-making muddle in which the CIA had become, at least on the all-important operating level, a power unto itself.

3. An ideological mixup in which the United States had become identified with the conservative exiled factions with the most support in Miami, and was regarded as hostile to the anti-Castro faction with the broadest support in Cuba.

Certainly the President can be criticized for approving the plan; but those responsible for initiating the venture in the first place seem scarcely in a position to fault Mr. Kennedy for badly finishing a project badly begun.

As the President reviewed the matter, the temptation to go ahead must have been irresistible, whatever his doubts about the over-all soundness of the plan. Recall that his chief intelligence and military advisers were united in endorsing the plan—and that the plan they were endorsing did not call for direct United States military intervention. If the decision to withold direct American support robbed the venture of a chance to succeed, then presumably it was the duty of the Joint Chiefs and the CIA to say just that.

Some argue that the President's aides—specifically the "new hands"—failed to do their duty by making their strenuous objections felt. But it was part of the web of circumstance that none of the men around Kennedy really knew very much about Cuba, Castro and guerrilla warfare. New to the world of secret intelligence reports, they credited the CIA with an acumen the Agency lacked.

Why didn't they object on principle, following Fulbright's lead? But the "new hands" were just that—new to their jobs—and were extremely uncertain of their ground in dealing with the President and fearful of seeming softheaded in an atmosphere of *realpolitik*. Suppose the experts were right? Wouldn't the lonely objector look foolish after the fact? The "new hands" were not made of the stuff of martyrs, wearing their ideals on rolled-up sleeves.

Thus, on that lonely night, the President made the most damaging and embarrassing decision· of his first year. The next day, he called a smaller meeting attended by Secretary Rusk, Secretary McNamara and Allen Dulles. He told them that the plan had won his final approval.

On April 12, the President made public the general lines of his decision. He told the news conference that not "under any conditions" would the United States directly participate in the coming showdown with Cuba. "The basic issue in Cuba is not one between the United States and Cuba," he explained, "it is between the Cubans themselves. I intend to see that we adhere to that principle." Some critics contended subsequently that the President erred grievously by invoking a principle that handcuffed him when the invasion foundered and when only direct U. S. intervention would have saved it.

The invasion was five days off.

IX

After it was over, the press and the public asked, "How did it happen?" In reviewing the chain of events between January and April, the question might properly be reversed! How could it have happened otherwise? Every link in the chain—the transitional confusion in government, the momentum of an operation already underway, the temperament of those who met behind closed doors—all seemed to predetermine "the disposal problem."

In the view of some who were involved, one factor might have altered the outcome. The American press, if it had fully and simply reported the facts, might have given an uncertain President the pretext he needed for scrapping or altering the basic character of the CIA plan.

But the press, like the President, also faced anguishing dilemmas in dealing with a venture unprecedented in American history. Here was an operation partly based on American soil, deeply involving the American Government, aimed at an objective that most Americans would approve—the elimination of Castro.

To report the invasion preparations and the pecadilloes of the CIA would be to compromise the Government and possibly jeopardize the success of the plan. Yet to ignore the news would be a disservice to readers and a breach of the lofty pretensions of a free press.

Some editors resolved the dilemma by becoming active accomplices of the CIA. This was especially true in Florida; at one point, a Philadelphia editor called up a Miami publisher to ask if the rumors about Guatemala training camps were true. He was told by his friend in Florida that there was nothing to the story.

Other papers took to hinting obliquely at what was going on. The first report on the Guatemala camps came in the unlikely pages of the *Hispanic-American Report,* a scholarly journal published by the Institute of Hispanic American Studies at Stanford University. This was in October 1960; Dr. Ronald Hilton of the Institute followed up with an article in the *Nation* in November. Earlier stories had appeared in *La Hora,* a Guatemala paper, written by Clemente Marroquín Rojas. On December 22, Donald Dwiggins, aviation editor of the Los Angeles *Mirror,* reported to his readers about the strange goings-on he encountered during a trip to Guatemala. At the same time, Richard Dudman of the St. Louis *Post-Dispatch* made a trip to Guatemala and confirmed the existence of the camps.

On January 6, 1961, *Time* carried a frank report that disclosed the exiles' maneuvers: "The underground Big Two are wide apart on politics and on who gets what funds. The Frente apparently gets virtually all U.S. financial aid to Cuba's underground (estimated to range from $135,000 monthly to as high as $500,000 on occasions), and 'Mr. B,' the CIA agent in charge, reportedly has suggested that the MRP get help from the Frente."

The most direct story appeared in the New York *Times* on January 10, by Paul Kennedy. It gave an account of United States help for the exiles' forces at the main Guatemalan base in Retalhuleu. This was followed by other reports from Miami as the invasion buildup began, reports that described what everyone in the city knew was going on. The stories revealed no secrets to Fidel Castro, but they did attempt to let the American people know what was going on. At this point the White House might have reasonably deduced that it would be impossible really to conceal United States participation.

By April, the essential elements of the CIA plan were known. On April 9, William V. Shannon, Washington correspondent of the New York *Post,* reported accurately that Cuba was about to get "the Guatemala treatment" and that the CIA had cast Captain Manuel Artime in the role of Colonel Castillo Armas. The April 8 edition of the *Saturday Evening Post* carried an article by Harold H. Martin that described the various exile factions and United States favoritism for the "Catholic, conservative and sternly anti-Communist" *Frente*.

Thus, by piecing together various reports, the careful reader could deduce what was happening. But he would have to tread warily through planted and inspired stories put out by insiders who favored the invasion—stories that told of Russian destroyers sailing to Cuba and of MIG fighters that were already being flown in Cuban skies.

After it was over, in the emotions of the moment, some

Administration spokesman was quick to blame the press for its alleged indiscretions in describing the invasion buildup. The argument was that press publicity stripped the cover from the United States operation and made it impossible for the Government to disassociate itself from a venture into the political black market.

Surely, in retrospect, the question takes a different shape. Was it the fault of the press that the CIA undertook to organize an army and form a government from American soil, using as much discretion as carnival shills before a sideshow tent? It was like plumping Disneyland in the middle of Times Square and then asking newspapermen to obligingly look the other way. After it was over, some of the same insiders who talked magazines and newspapers out of running factual articles on the CIA venture conceded that they wished the editors hadn't listened. If there is any utility in freedom of the press, it is precisely that the press can act as an independent corrective on the blunders of government. With the best and most patriotic intentions, a great many newspapermen and some Administration officials failed to rely on the very principles of freedom for which the Cuban invaders were ready to die.

This, then, was the clinching link in the chain as "the disposal problem" was about to be definitely solved.

CHAPTER SEVEN

ON THE BEACH

Shortly after six o'clock on the morning of Saturday, April 15, the population of Havana was awakened by the roar of low-flying aircraft, scattered bomb explosions, and the bark of anti-aircraft artillery. Looking up, the *Habaneros* could see a pair of B-26 bombers with the insignia of Castro's FAR—the Revolutionary Air Force—making diving passes at the Camp Libertad airfield on the outskirts of the city. A few minutes earlier, the attacking bombers had strafed the big air force base at San Antonio de los Baños, not far from Havana. A third B-26 made passes about an hour later over the airfield at Santiago in the eastern province of Oriente.

Militarily, air strike number one was not effective. It was

the prelude to the invasion that was to come 48 hours later, although the puzzle remains as to the strategic sense of a softening-up raid on a Saturday in preparation for an amphibious attack planned for Monday. The chief effect was to alert Castro that the long-awaited invasion was imminent.

The objective of the raid was to destroy on the ground as many Castro aircraft as possible so that the invaders on Monday would not be subject to air attack. It was believed that the Cubans had about fifteen B-26's, which Castro inherited from Batista, three T-33 jet trainers, and a half-dozen British-built Sea Fury light attack bombers. CIA reports had indicated that Castro had a certain number of Soviet MIG fighters, but it was not known whether the planes had been taken out of their crates and made operational.

The air attack was to be the last preparatory touch before the landings. Early in April, as the operation was about to be set in motion, the CIA had made another attempt to weaken the Cuban defenses, but it too was largely unsuccessful. This effort involved a plan in which a number of Cuban torpedo boats, many of them fast craft built in East Germany, would escape from the naval base of Baracoa in Oriente Province and make a dash for freedom. Anti-Castro elements in the Cuban navy had advised that this would be possible, provided that the torpedo boats could be refueled on the high seas, since the political unreliability of the crews caused the regime to keep the craft on short gasoline ration.

Several boats escaped to Haiti on their own in late March, whereupon the Cubans reduced the fuel ration even further. To help the potential defectors, a privately owned undersea-cable repair ship, the *Western Union,* put in at Guantánamo to load on her deck several thousand drums of high-octane gasoline. But on her way to the Baracoa rendezvous, the vessel was intercepted by a Cuban warship. Anguished radio messages to Guantánamo sent a United States destroyer and Navy aircraft rushing toward the *Western Union,* and, in the end, the Cuban captain let himself be stared down by the American forces and allowed the cable ship to go. Once discovered, however, the *Western Union* could no longer pursue her mission and she sheepishly sailed to Key West, Florida, where Federal agents prevented the captain from speaking to newsmen.

Meanwhile, the final preparations for the attack were underway. A general mobilization of the rebels was ordered in Miami by the Cuban Revolutionary Council about April 1, and volunteers drove nightly to the building of the Democratic Front in Coral Gables to report for duty. They were accompanied by weeping relatives who parted from them in tearful scenes, handing the soldiers paper bags of sandwiches and cold chicken. Scores of Cuban doctors and nurses who had earlier volunteered for duty were notified to depart for a hospital ship that was being outfitted somewhere in Florida, and for medical units in Guatemala. Surgical supply stores in Miami were virtually emptied by Cubans.

From the Front's offices, the volunteers were driven in trucks to the Opa-Locka airport, placed aboard unmarked transport aircraft and flown to Guatemala. Before boarding the planes, they were issued khaki uniforms and were deprived of their own clothes and all identification. These were the security measures being taken by the CIA to conceal the mobilization, but they were about as effective as concealing an elephant with a bath towel. The mobilization was a public spectacle, the families were fully aware of what was happening, and only sublimely unobservant Castro agents in Miami could have failed to report all the details.

About ten days before the invasion, at least one newspaper correspondent in Miami was notified by Cuban friends that the attack would be launched on April 18, a guess that was only a day off. The deduction was sensibly based on advance orders to exile broadcasting stations to leave the air on April 18 so that the frequencies would be available for operational communications.

So feverish was the atmosphere that the CIA relented and began to supply some equipment to Manuel Ray's long-neglected MRP underground. Ray had been named coordinator of the Revolutionary Council's underground activities and at last felt his arguments were making an impact. Navy planes from the Key West naval station flew cover over the international waters for the MRP speedboats carrying explosives and weapons.

Thus encouraged, and sensing that an attack was near, the underground moved into action during the week of April 10. Explosions shook Havana, as the city's largest and closely guarded department store, El Encanto, went up in flames. The big Hershey sugar mill was also burned, along with a large wholesale house in Santiago. MRP leaders in Miami were promising a major sabotage campaign as soon as a shipment of two tons of C-4 plastic explosives—the best available—was received in Cuba. It appeared that a well thought out softening-up process had begun and that the

118

Cuban underground, now displaying its effectiveness, would be brought into the operation.

Ray and his military adviser, Colonel Ramón Barquín, talked of several weeks of mounting sabotage, culminating in a series of multiple landings by guerilla forces coordinated with uprisings by the underground. This, they said, would be a victorious "war of liberation" and not a "war of conquest" that would be bound to create resentment in Cuba and throughout Latin America. Some CIA agents hinted that this was indeed the plan, and in Washington stories based on high Administration sources asserted that the United States was determined to avoid all appearance of a "Hungary in reverse."

But by this time the CIA had already made the decision for a one-thrust invasion. Earlier plans calling for multiple attacks coupled with internal insurrection were scrapped when the CIA concluded that the underground in Cuba could not be supplied properly by air and therefore could not be built into a reliable force. By a circular process, the CIA was in a position to discourage the growth of the underground and then cite the very lack of growth as the reason for minimizing the role of internal resistance. A second argument was that the underground was not sufficiently "security" conscious and thus could not be trusted—even though the CIA evidently trusted the equally loquacious Cubans in Miami. In the end, the CIA failed to alert the Cuban underground and went all out for one big invasion; even the diversionary strike by a commando group on the coasts of Oriente and Pinar del Río provinces never materialized because of confused directives and operational breakdowns.

Early in the week of April 10, Operation Pluto entered the final phase. Captain Artime was named the military delegate of the Revolutionary Council to the camps. Manuel Ray, who was beginning to sense disaster, saw the appointment as a violation of the pact which set up the Council. The choice of Artime meant the passing over of Colonel Ramón Barquín, an experienced officer with impeccable democratic credentials who had been jailed by Batista—and who had insistently warned of the folly of an all-or-nothing invasion. Ray considered pulling out of the Council altogether, but in the interests of unity he finally agreed to stay.

That week, the Guatemalan camps began to be emptied as unmarked United States aircraft ferried the rebel troops to Puerto Cabezas, Nicaragua, where they were visisted by President Luis Somoza before boarding the invasion ships. Besides the men, about fifty freight carloads of aerial bombs, rockets, firearms and ammunition were airlifted to the port. A force of 150 guerrilla fighters commanded by Major Nino Díaz was ordered to standby for a landing on the coast of Oriente Province in a diversionary movement. Guerrilla specialists from a camp in Louisiana were flown to Puerto Cabezas. At Vieques Island, the United States Marine Corps amphibious warfare reservation off Puerto Rico, Cuban rebel frogmen and underwater demolition experts prepared to join the main force. In Miami, the Council's radio operators exchanged messages with Artime's headquarters in Guatemala and then in Nicaragua. Wives, mothers and sisters of the rebel soldiers flocked to the Miami churches to pray for the success of the invasion.

Everybody, it seemed, was in on the secret and knew the details except the hapless Revolutionary Council in whose name the war was to be fought. On Thursday, April 13, the entire Council was invited to New York by the CIA and quartered at the Hotel Lexington for a series of conferences. On Friday night, they were told that an air strike would occur the next morning. Dr. Miró Cardona tossed sleeplessly, awaiting the results.

The results proved to be disappointing. The B-26's took off from Guatemala during the night for their hit-and-run raids on Havana, San Antonio de los Baños and Santiago. However, they failed to accomplish their mission of knocking out Castro's own air force and veered over the northern coast and set course for Florida, their tanks virtually empty.

The first bomber landed at Key West Naval Air Station at 7 a.m. on April 15, with one of its engines feathered. It carried two pilots. At 8:20 a.m., the second bomber came down at the Miami International Airport, one of its engines also feathered and its wings and fuselage riddled with bullets. The second B-26 carried only one pilot.

No sooner had the two aircraft landed than they were involved in a mist of contradictory stories. Castro promptly charged that the bombers had come from foreign bases, but the Revolutionary Council, sitting in New York, issued a communiqué announcing that the B-26's had been flown out of Cuba by defecting Castro airmen who decided to inflict a little damage before escaping the island. The Council said that six aircraft, including a T-33 jet trainer, were involved, and that one of the "defecting" planes had been shot down.

Late in the afternoon, Immigration Service officials issued a statement attributed to the pilot who landed in Miami to the effect that he was one of four Castro fliers who had planned to defect three months ago. The man was quoted as saying

120

that the plan was precipitated when he and two other companions discovered two days before that the fourth airman had been talking to Castro's secret police and might have betrayed the plot. The confused statement indicated that three B-26's were involved, but since two other pilots were already accounted for, it was not clear who flew the third bomber. No attempt was made to square the pilot's story with the Council's statement that six aircraft were involved.

The Immigration Service refused to identify the pilot, but his photograph, showing his face clearly under a flier's cap, appeared in the early evening edition of a Miami newspaper. Other photographs showed the plane in painstaking detail.

Although the CIA had taken the pains to disguise the B-26 with "FAR" markings, the agency overlooked a crucial detail that was spotted immediately by professional observers who saw the bomber at the airport or in the newspaper photographs. This was the fact that while Castro's B-26's were equipped with plexiglass noses, the aircraft given the rebel pilots were models with opaque noses.

It did not take much time for a group of pilots in Miami who had served in Guatemala to recognize the "defector" as one of their companions from the secret camps. Before night fell, it was common knowledge in Miami that the "defector" was a Lieutenant Zuñiga. His wife also saw the newspaper picture and telephoned a friend to inquire where she could find her husband, whom she had not seen since he left for Guatemalan camps several months before.

Did the CIA expect this flimsy deceit to succeed? All Castro had to do to establish whether any of his pilots or planes had defected was to find out whether any men or equipment were missing.

In the end, ironically, the raid itself was a cruel deception. Reports had been sent to Washington describing the raid as successful, when it wasn't, and this report, tied in with other events, led to the cancellation of a second strike planned for early Monday to assure the complete destruction of Castro's air power. Here we encounter the crowning paradox of the invasion plan. The hundred elaborate wheels turned smoothly to organize the landing force, but one small cog—essential to the movement of the entire machine—fell out of place. The fact that the second strike did not take place was one of the keys of the military failure of the entire plan.

By this time, the invasion plans had passed the point of no return, even if any one had been disposed to postpone or cancel the attack. The rebel army was already aboard the ships, sailing from Nicaragua, under the cover of a squadron of United States destroyers that led the pathetic little armada of old cargo ships and landing craft toward the Cuban shore to a by now predetermined destiny.

On Saturday night, "Tony" Varona, who was nominally the "War Minister" in the Revolutionary Council, flew hurriedly from New York to Miami for last-minute consultations. He returned to New York on Sunday morning, just in time for a lunchtime conference of the Council in a suite on the tenth floor of the Lexington Hotel.

Early in the afternoon, the Council was advised that important events were forthcoming and that for reasons of general security, and in order to be ready to return to Cuba, the Council had to slip out of sight. Led by Frank Bender and escorted by ten CIA agents, the members of the Council, still ignorant of what was about to happen, were shepherded downstairs through a back elevator and taken to waiting cars. After a three-hour drive, they arrived at the Philadelphia airport, where they boarded a plane operated by the Immigration Service.

By evening, the aircraft landed at Opa-Locka, just outside Miami. The members of the Council were led to a house on the outskirts of the field. CIA agents armed with rifles guarded the house. Dinner was served to the Council, and each member was issued a duffle bag containing a rebel uniform and campaign equipment.

When members of the Cuban Revolutionary Council inquired about what was occurring, Bender and his aides shook their heads, professing ignorance. It was midnight when the Council members finally went to sleep.

At that moment, the invasion ships were edging close to the coast of the Bay of Pigs.

II

The scene shifts from the demimonde of the "black" service and the mobilization tumult in Miami and Havana to a gleaming glass house on the East River in New York where the follies of government become the stuff of debate. The place is the modernistic auditorium in which the United Nations Political Committee is meeting. The time is Saturday morning, April 15.

Raúl Roa, Cuba's Foreign Minister, whose spectacles invariably seem about to slither off his nose, is speaking. "I have been instructed by my government," Roa tells the crowded room, "to denounce before this committee the vandalistic aggression carried out at dawn today against the territorial

122

integrity of Cuba, with the most grave implication. The responsibility for this act of imperialistic piracy falls squarely on the government of the United States."

The Cuban paused, the room buzzed with talk as Roa resumed to charge that the incident "undoubtedly is the prelude to a large-scale invasion attempt, organized, supplied and financed by the United States with the complicity of satellite dictatorships of the Western Hemisphere."

In tense confrontation, Adlai Stevenson began his reply, confident that the information he had received about the raid was true. The Ambassador of the United States held a photograph of one of the planes that had landed in Florida. "It has the markings of Castro's air force on the tail," Stevenson asserted, pointing to the picture, "which everybody can see for himself. The Cuban star and the initials FAR—Fuerza Aerea Revolucionaria—are clearly visible. The two aircraft which landed in Florida today . . . were piloted by Cuban air force pilots. These pilots and certain other crew members have apparently defected from Castro's tyranny. No United States personnel participated. No United States government planes of any kind participated. These two planes to the best of our knowledge were Castro's own air force planes, and, according to the pilots, they took off from Castro's own air force fields."

With the firmness that springs from conviction, Stevenson turned to the committee and summed up his case: "As President Kennedy said just a few days ago, the basic issue in Cuba is not between the United States and Cuba, it is between the Cubans themselves. . . . The history of Cuba has been a history of fighting for freedom. Regardless of what happens, the Cubans will fight for freedom. The activities of the last 24 hours are an eloquent confirmation of this historical fact."

An ambassador, it is said, is an honest man sent to lie for his commonwealth. But Stevenson had not only been forced to lie, he had thought he was speaking the truth. The man who had to defend the attack before the United Nations was not told the facts about the raid; instead he was given a "cover story" so flimsy that the Cubans were able immediately to place the United States in an excruciatingly embarrassing position.

On Sunday, Castro took the offensive, calling the attack "Cuba's Pearl Harbor," and accurately predicting that its purpose was to destroy the Cuban air force as a prelude to aggression. In a two-hour speech delivered at fever pitch at a military funeral for those killed in the raid, Castro cried, "If President Kennedy has one atom of decency, he will present the planes and pilots before the United Nations. If not, then the world has a right to call him a liar."

For the first time in public, Castro described his revolution as socialistic. Washington officials could not forgive him, he said, for making "a socialist revolution right under their noses." He added that his people would defend this "revolution of the humble, by the humble and for the humble to the last drop of blood." His paraphrase of Lincoln brought forth shouts: "Fidel, Khrushchev, we are with both!"

The United Nations imbroglio prompted a swirl of meetings and frantic messages involving Stevenson, Secretary of State Rusk, White House aid McGeorge Bundy, and the President. A dozen different versions circulate as to who said what to whom. Notwithstanding the conflicting testimony, the outcome was that the President canceled the second air strike planned to assure that Castro's air power was knocked out. To what extent faulty intelligence reports on the first strike contributed to his decision is not known at this time.

Stevenson did not know about the planned second raid, and authoritative accounts insist that he had no direct part in the cancellation. But his reaction to being badly used did play a part in the decision. He was furious, and surely with reason. The President was shaken by Stevenson's reaction.

In an article in the September 1961 issue of *Fortune*, Charles J. V. Murphy has elaborated the thesis that this last-minute shift, along with other hasty revisions in the details of the plan, doomed the invasion. Clearly, the changes did not improve Operation Pluto's chances for success, but so many mistakes of every order—military, political and psychological—played a part in the debacle that to emphasize a single bad decision might leave the impression that everything else was "sound."

Mr. Murphy ignores, for example, a defect more fundamental than the cancellation of an air strike employing a crude deceit more worthy of the communists and Castro than the United States. This was the total failure to work with the Cuban underground. Viewed strictly as a military venture, the single most mystifying fact about the CIA plan is that it excluded the Cuban people as untrustworthy allies. Many post-mortems have lamented the so-called "political" considerations that led the President to hold back United States military forces. But the political consideration that seems more crucial had less to do with world opinion than Cuban opinion. The role of the Cubans in the plan was that of stooges, not partners; no provision was made for those gallant Cubans who might want to liberate themselves.

A few days before the invasion, the "National Coordinator" of the Cuban underground was smuggled out of Cuba and taken to New York for sessions with the Revolutionary Council. He presented a plan which called for a concentrated sabotage campaign in April, with Havana power plants, major highways and railroads as the main targets. He was supplied with two tons of powerful C-4 plastic explosions and was ordered back to Cuba.

But he was not told that the date of the invasion had been set and that the armada was being assembled in Puerto Cabezas. He was fast asleep in a modest Miami home when the news of the invasion came at dawn. His voice broke when he asked one of the authors on the telephone at 5 a.m., "Do you really mean that the invasion has started without us?"

It had indeed.

III

The event itself was accompanied by romantic flourishes in the best cloak-and-dagger tradition. As the flotilla was assembling for the strike, a clandestine radio transmitter sent suitably baffling messages into the Caribbean sky: "Alert! Alert! Look well at the rainbow. The first will rise very soon. Chico is in the house. Visit him. The sky is blue. Place notice in the tree. The tree is green and brown. The letters arrived well. The letters are white. The fish will not take much time to rise. The fish is red. Look well at the rainbow. . . ."

By one o'clock on the morning of April 17, the invasion fleet, composed of four cargo ships and two LCI's (Landing Craft Infantry), and assisted by nearly a dozen smaller landing craft, took positions off the coast of Las Villas Province. The targets were two beaches—Playa Girón, known operationally as the Blue Beach, and Playa Larga, known as the Green Beach—located respectively at the entrance of the Bay of Pigs and at its apex.

The bay jutted into the swamps of Ciénaga de Zapata, a marshy peninsula in the south of Cuba, but there was firm ground at the beaches where the Castro regime had built resorts for the workers. Good hard-surfaced roads led inland to connect with the Cuban highway network. The wild shoreline was exotic, resembling the Florida Everglades, and the night air was buffeted by a breeze from the north. The crescent moon had already set; the only sound was the splash of fish and alligators and the rustle of tropical birds. Deep in the swamp, Castro himself had built a tin-roofed fishing cabin, about two hours march from the landing area.

At 1:15 a.m., Radio Swan, the CIA-controlled station, beamed to Cuba a statement issued in the name of José Miró Cardona: "Before dawn Cuban patriots in the cities and in the hills began the battle to liberate our homeland from the despotic rule of Fidel Castro. . . . In their unquenchable thirst for liberty the Cuban people today seize arms to obliterate a vicious alien oppressor fired by the vision of inevitable victory, and convinced that the freedom-loving peoples of this hemisphere will make common cause with them. . . ." In the United States, the statement was mimeographed and released as "Bulletin No. 1" by Lem Jones Associates, Inc., 280 Madison Avenue, New York, the public-relations firm employed to "handle" the Cuban invasion.

The battle was joined; the following account is based on both interviews with the prisoners and survivors and on Castro's own detailed account, which has been confirmed by participants as substantially accurate, although there are discrepancies that will be noted.

A few minutes before 2 a.m., frogmen slid into the water from speedboats lowered by one of the assault crafts, and swam to the two beaches to install position lights and destroy any obstacles to the landing. Between 2:30 a.m. and 3 a.m., two batallions of the rebel brigade came ashore at Playa Girón and one batallion landed at Playa Larga. The armada's five tanks were rolled ashore at Playa Girón, with orders to proceed along the coastal highway and link up with troops further north at Playa Larga, thereby securing a long beachhead. A small column was sent to the north toward the town of Jaguey Grande, which had a small airstrip.

As the invaders waded onto the beach and through the mangrove swamps, they encountered little initial resistance. Small militia units guarding the beaches were easily overcome and a few residents of the area joined the attacking force and were given weapons. All together, an entire miniature army was dumped on the shore, with 867.8 tons of supplies and weapons for 4,000 men. The extra arms were for "friendly forces" which were expected to join with the invaders.

The news of the landing found Castro in Havana, where he heard by telephone from Jagüey Grande that the invasion was on. Immediately, the Premier alerted his tiny air force and his large army and sped toward the invasion area, setting up his field headquarters at the Australia sugar mill, north of

Playa Larga, and then at Treasure Lagoon, a few miles to the south.

At daybreak, Castro's aircraft roared into the sky under strict orders to concentrate on rebel shipping and to ignore the battlefield. That first day, Castro had available only two T-33 jet trainers, two Sea Furies and two B-26's. The rest of his air force was immobilized for lack of spare parts, according to subsequent Cuban accounts. But he knew how to use his six aircraft, and his resourcefulness was decisive in winning a quick victory.

Shuttling between the San Antonio base on the northern coast and the invasion area, his pilots displayed considerable ability, but they were abetted by luck. At 6:45 a.m., Captain Enrique Carreras Rolas, a 38-year-old pilot, flew his Sea Fury toward the 3,000-ton cargo ship *Houston* (also known as the *Aguja*), and hit it with four five-inch rockets. The *Houston* carried the 5th Batallion of the brigade, most of the communications equipment, and Captain Artime.

At the time, the *Houston* was proceeding toward Playa Larga to disgorge her cargo. Hit in her prow, the ship ran aground on a sandspit two miles from the beach. Within the hour, the LCI known as *Marsopa,* which had acted as the control ship for the operation, was sunk by other pilots, along with eight other small landing craft. Before 8 a.m., therefore, the armada had already been seriously damaged.

Meanwhile, some 175 paratroopers had been dropped inland to secure control of the access roads to the beachhead. It was Premier Castro's opinion, when he toured the battlefield with one of the authors in July 1961, that the paratroopers had been dropped too close to the battlefield to be really useful in cutting off communications—and, indeed, during the battle their prime concern became fighting their way to the beachhead.

In other respects, Castro said he thought the choice of the landing area was excellent and that it came as a surprise to him, although he was expecting the invasion that day. The strategic concept, Castro felt, was sound in theory: the coast was lightly defended and a sudden landing offered a reasonable chance for establishing a fair-sized beachhead before the defenders could bring reinforcements from other parts of Cuba. But the expansion of the beachhead would have been possible only if Castro had been blocked from sending reinforcements from his army of 250,000. The underground, which might have performed this task, was excluded from the operation. Diversionary landings were also not carried out, enabling Castro to bring the full force of his militia to bear on a slim beachhead held by some 1,500 troops.

By 8 a.m., Castro had ordered into action an understrength militia batallion from the Australia sugar mill, while another batallion advanced from Cienfuegos. Other militia units from neighboring Matanzas Province were ordered toward the battlefield, and, in Havana, tanks and artillery were being loaded on flatbed trucks to be rushed to the invasion area.

In the air, the paratroop drop was followed by a flight of B-26's that strafed and bombed Castro troops on the ground. In the day's combat, the invaders quickly had five of their twelve B-26's shot down, while Castro lost a Sea Fury and a B-26. The swifter moving T-33 trainer jets gave Castro a crucial advantage in felling the lumbering B-26's.

During the course of the first day of battle, the rebel brigade moved about twenty miles inland and held 43 miles of the coast. This was the peak of its success before the tide turned. The invaders never had a chance; despite their extensive training and their elaborate equipment, the rebel brigades were exposed to relentless air attack and had virtually no indigenous support within the island to hamper Castro's massive counterstrokes. Already it became clear, on the first day, that the invasion force could not be resupplied. Supplies could neither be flown in nor transported from floating depots. The major supply ships had to stay out of range of Castro's jets.

There was a pathetic footnote as the first day was drawing to a close. The taped voice of Captain Manuel Artime, the erstwhile golden boy of the CIA, was heard over Miami's WMET. Introduced as "Commander in Chief of the Army of Liberation," the 29-year-old, little-known Cuban was solemnly proclaiming: "I, Manuel Artime, convoke the Cuban people to revolt in fulfillment of my promise of a year ago." By that time, Artime himself was somewhere in the dark swamps amid the shambles of the Bay of Pigs. Later, he was taken prisoner.

The confusion on the beachhead had a fitting counterpart in the misadventures of a small group of guerrilla fighters who were supposed to mount a diversionary attack in Oriente Province. The odyssey of this wandering army was so typical of the entire effort that it warrants a brief description.

According to the CIA plan, Major Nino Díaz was to take a contingent of 152 men to the eastern coast of Cuba and join with defectors to set up a guerrilla front. Major Díaz had once fought with Castro's rebel army in the Sierra Maestra and he knew—and was known in—Oriente Province.

A week before the invasion, his men boarded an ancient and rickety light cargo ship of the type used to ship bananas. The vessel flew a Costa Rican flag and the Díaz guerrillas were disguised in the garb of Castro's rebel army. Morale was high, even though there had been the usual dissension during the training period over the admission of Batista officers into the guerrilla force. The core of the unit was provided by fifty seasoned guerrilla fighters; the rest had been sent by the CIA to increase the size of the force. About a third of the men had received only a week's military training before boarding the ship. At embarkation time, the members of the force knew nothing about the April 17 invasion plan.

Stealthily, the craft headed for Cuba. By April 14—three days before the invasion—Díaz was poised to land at 10 p.m. at an uninhabited coastal spot between the cities of Baracoa and Guantánamo. The prearranged plan called for Díaz, to send a small boat near the shore to await a signal light from the underground. But to the surprise of Díaz, instead of a few signal flashes, the shore blazed with inviting lights. Suspicious of a trap, he waited until the following day to try again. This time it became clear that Castro's militia had been forewarned and was waiting to spring in the darkness on the guerrillas. Jeeps filled with militiamen could be seen on the roadway leading to the shore.

Díaz radioed to Guatemala and reported that it would be suicidal to land at the designated place. His first orders were to land anyway; Díaz refused. Then his creaking ship was ordered to another part of the island to join up with the main invading force. On April 17, in the morning, the Díaz guerrillas heard by radio that the Bay of Pigs "is ours" and were told to await offshore for instructions. The tiny army was jubilant, even though food and water had by this time run dangerously low.

Then came the bizarre twist. Two ships from the invasion armada came within sight of Díaz's craft—but the "regular" invaders were apparently confused by the encounter with a ship flying a Costa Rican flag and loaded with soldiers wearing Castro uniforms. The two "regular" ships bore down on Díaz, and the startled guerrillas soon became aware of the confusion of identity and in consternation began preparing to fight against their own side. Díaz's men desperately signaled and shouted, but to no avail. At the last moment, however, contact was made by walkie-talkie and an armed clash averted.

Subsequently, the Díaz guerrillas learned the truth about the invasion's failure and the ancient cargo ship began heading toward Key West, Florida. Headquarters in Guatemala radioed Díaz and told him to keep away from Key West because the

129

press was there. The homeless army changed course and then encountered a U. S. Navy destroyer. An argument ensued between the naval commander and Díaz, whose troops were by now thirsty, hungry and totally demoralized. Finally, the 152 wandering troops—still wearing their Castro-style uniforms—boarded the destroyer and were taken to Vieques Island, the U. S. Marine reservation off Puerto Rico. Members of the brigade still muse about how close they came to firing on fellow freedom fighters during the invasion melee.

V

The news of the invasion came with shuddering impact to Miami, where Cuban exiles huddled around radios; to Havana, where secret police began herding opposition suspects; and to an unbelieving world that followed the confused accounts of the battle.

In New York, at 4 a.m., Lem Jones Associates issued the second war bulletin on behalf of the Revolutionary Council. The communiqué was telephoned to Mr. Jones by a former Cuban judge who, in turn, received it from the CIA. It went as follows:

THE CUBAN REVOLUTIONARY COUNCIL
Via: Lem Jones Associates, Inc.
280 Madison Avenue
New York, New York
ORegon 9-5636
FOR IMMEDIATE RELEASE
April 17, 1961
Bulletin No. 2:

The Cuban Revolutionary Council announces a successful landing of military supplies and equipment in the Cochinos Bay area of Matanzas Province.

Overcoming some armed resistance by Castro supporters, substantial amounts of food and ammunition reached elements of internal resistance engaged in active combat.

For many months various revolutionary groups now integrated in the Cuban Revolutionary Council have been distributing a variety of revolutionary supplies and equipment to selected sites in Cuba.

The remote, thinly populated Zapata Marsh area of Matanzas Province has served as a zone in which munitions and equipment were cached for eventual use by resistance fighters in the Escambray and elsewhere.

Because Cuban Revolutionary Council members are now totally occupied with the dramatic events unfolding in Cuba, their views will be made known to the press solely through the Cuban Revolutionary Council's spokesman, Dr. Antonio Silió.

Indeed, the Revolutionary Council was "totally occupied" with the drama. The members of the Council were trying to find out what was happening in the war they were supposed to be leading but did not even know had begun. Penned up in a deserted house near Opa-Locka airfield, Council members first heard about the invasion when one of the Cubans happened to turn on a radio and heard a Miami newscast quoting from the dawn proclamation issued in the Council's name. Bender told the questioning Cubans to stand by and be ready to fly to the beachhead and establish a "Government in Arms."

In Miami itself, the Cuban community was pulsing with excitement. Within hours after the attack, reports were circulating of imminent victory and of attacks all over the island of Cuba. The first evening editions of the Miami press displayed maps of Cuba showing imaginary pincer movements by rebel forces and carried detailed descriptions of wild battles written by reporters who spared not an adjective in describing a war they never saw.

As newsmen poured into Miami hotels—the closest spot to the beachhead—agents for the Revolutionary Council began signing them up for trips to the battlefront. In mounting excitement, reporters pored over a third bulletin from Lem Jones, which said:

CUBAN REVOLUTIONARY COUNCIL
Via: Lem Jones Associates, Inc.
280 Madison Avenue
New York, New York
ORegon 9-5636
FOR IMMEDIATE RELEASE
April 17, 1961
7:15 p.m.

Bulletin No. 3:

The Cuban Revolutionary Council wishes to announce that the principal battle of the Cuban revolt against Castro will be fought in the next few hours. Action today was largely of a supply and support effort to forces which have been mobilized and trained inside Cuba over the past several months.

The tremendous army of invisible soldier-patriots has now received its instructions to strike the vital blow for the liberation of their beloved country.

Our partisans in every town and village in Cuba will receive, in a manner known only to them, the message which will spark a tremendous wave of internal conflict against the tyrant. The spokesman for the Revolutionary Council stated:

"I predict that before dawn the island of Cuba will rise up en masse in a coordinated wave of sabotage and rebellion which will sweep communism from our country."

It is obvious that details of these events which are about to happen can not be made public here. However, it can be revealed that the patriots have been instructed to cut communications, destroy power facilities, disrupt transportation and mobilize against Castro.

Furthermore, it is expected before dawn Cuban patriots will move against the ever dwindling portion of the militia which has not already come over to our side.

Our information from Cuba indicates that much of the militia in the countryside has already defected from Castro.

As was indicated in the press of April 16, our clandestine radio has been giving instructions to the insurgents throughout the island. In a coded message, on this radio yesterday, a statement was made that "the fish will soon stand."

As is well known the fish is the Christian symbol of resistance. When the fish is placed in a vertical position it is a sign that internal revolt is in full swing. The fish will stand tonight!

Standing or not, Mr. Lem Jones himself was before a microphone that Monday evening. On the 11 p.m. CBS news program, an interviewing reporter explained that Mr. Jones had specialized in stock-proxy fights, and the publicist was asked if he saw any resemblance between handling an invasion and a stock battle. Mr. Jones, a bit embarrassed, replied that perhaps there might be some analogy because both fights involved an "insurgent" element and an entrenched management.

In Havana, the entrenched management was not idle in resisting the insurgents. After the April 15 raid, Castro deliberately kept popular feeling calm by playing music on government stations—at the time that the CIA station inexplicably went silent. The day of the invasion, beginning at 8 a.m., the local radio stations started broadcasting "urgent" calls from the general staff of the army ordering all militiamen to report at once to their units. At 11:07 a.m., the radios carried a proclamation signed by Castro and President Dorticós declaring that Cuba had been attacked and announcing a national alert. The only official word on the fighting came in a morning proclamation declaring that "our troops are advancing against the enemy . . . in the certainty of victory." The regime's internal microwave network broadcasts revealed that Castro had been under air attack at Treasure Lagoon early in the morning, but few other details were available, except for an avalanche of orders.

While Cuban troops were moving against the beachhead, Castro's secret police began a massive roundup of suspected counterrevolutionaries. In the wholesale arrests that, by evening, filled every prison on the island as well as Havana's sports arena and several theaters, most of the underground found itself under detention along with thousands of uninvolved bystanders. The failure to alert the underground extinguished whatever slim chance existed for an uprising.

The G-2 cast a wide net; among those arrested were old-time American residents, United States newsmen, and even Havana's Bishop, Msgr. Eduardo Boza Masvidal, who was detained during the afternoon.

As night fell, Castro's forces had surrounded the beachhead, established control of the air, prevented any blockage of communications, and placed most opposition elements elsewhere on the island under arrest.

No less important, if Castro was militarily strong at home, the circumstances of the invasion brought him important support from abroad. News-agency cables were humming with dispatches from all corners of the earth, and most of the reports were adverse to the United States. In Bogotá, 1,000 demonstrators stoned the United States Embassy, shouting, predictably, "Cuba sí, Yankee no!"; in New Delhi, the press and government were quick to express disapproval; in Buenos Aires, Castro supporters heaved tarballs at the USIA office; in Great Britain, the Manchester Guardian, renowned for its principled dissent during the Suez war, grieved that Kennedy "has sailed too near the water for no good reason"; in Caracas, the legislature unanimously passed a resolution condemning "any armed intervention in Cuba or in any other American country," and—most ominously—in Moscow, Tass reported that "Cuba is not alone." Shortly,

133

there were mobs before the American Embassy in Moscow, crying, *"Cuba da, Yankee nyet!"*

At the United Nations, Ambassador Stevenson was in a defensive and difficult position, but, with dignity, he tried to put the best face on matters. In answer to the Cuban charge of direct intervention, Stevenson stressed a technical distinction: "No offensive had been launched from Florida or from any other part of the United States." In reply to accusations by Foreign Minister Roa that the invaders were hired mercenaries, the American Ambassador replied tartly: "Many of them are Dr. Roa's friends and associates of long standing. They make a rather impressive list: the first Provisional President of the Revolutionary Government, Dr. Manuel Urrutia; the first Prime Minister, Dr. José Miró Cardona; the first President of the Supreme Court, Dr. Emilio Menéndez." Throughout, Stevenson reiterated one theme. "What Roa seeks from us today," he asserted, "is protection for a terroristic regime from the natural wrath of the Cuban people."

For his part, Foreign Minister Roa had one major argument that he embroidered in a dozen patterns: "The government of the United States has exported war to us. . . . My heroic country is proving again the story of David against Goliath." And, notwithstanding Mr. Stevenson's eloquence, that was how millions of people in the world saw it.

VI

The day began early for President John F. Kennedy, the American most keenly concerned with the battle on the Bay of Pigs.

At 5:15 a.m. on Monday, Brigadier General Chester Clifton, the President's military adviser, heard by telephone that the invasion had begun. He told his informant to call Mr. Kennedy at the President's weekend retreat in Glen Ora, Virginia. By 5:30, the President was up and around, and he soon turned up at the White House to study the first fragmentary reports. They were not encouraging.

Secretary of State Rusk, at his regular news conference, which came a few hours after the first invasion reports, made the first official statement on the event. "There is no secret about the sympathy of the American people for those who wish to be free," he said, adding with emphasis: "What happens in Cuba is for the Cuban people themselves to decide." Rusk declined to answer any questions about United

134

States material, training or financial assistance to the invaders, but stressed that "there is not now and will not be any intervention there by United States forces." From what he had seen of press reports, the soft-spoken Secretary observed, he would not characterize the action "as a large-scale invasion."

The day progressed, and by sundown the gloom was already evident. No discernible uprisings had yet occurred and the militia was apparently fighting for Castro. That evening, Adolf A. Berle, Jr., had a few select friends for dinner at his Georgetown home when a message came that cast a pall on the gathering. The news was discouraging to those who had access to candid dispatches rather than the extravagant press accounts of multiple landings, mass defections and bloody uprisings—laced with planted rumors about various eminent Cubans killing themselves or being captured by wrathful insurgents.

Tuesday began with the President's regular breakfast meeting with congressional leaders. One legislator asked Mr. Kennedy what the chances were for success. "Forty per cent," the President replied, adding that much depended on the degree of support the invaders received from the Cuban people. Another question concerned a note that Premier Khrushchev had sent to Washington. The President replied that he doubted the Russians would send "volunteers."

The Khrushchev note was firmly worded: "As to the Soviet Union, there should be no misunderstanding our position. We shall render the Cuban people and their government all necessary assistance in beating back the armed attack on Cuba." That afternoon, the President set aside a reply drafted by the State Department and dictated his own answer. At around 7 p.m., the reply was handed to Mikhail A. Menshikov, the Soviet Ambassador to the United States. The note began: "You are under a serious misapprehension in regard to the events in Cuba . . ." and quickly came to the point: "I have previously stated, and I repeat now, that the United States intends no military intervention in Cuba. In the event of any military intervention by outside forces we will immediately honor our obligations under the inter-American system to protect this hemisphere against external aggression." It concluded:

I believe, Mr. Chairman, that you should recognize that free peoples do not accept the claim of historical inevitability for Communist revolutions. What your

135

government believes is its own business; what it does in the world is the world's business. The great revolution in the history of man, past, present and future, is the revolution of those determined to be free.

During the afternoon, Arthur M. Schlesinger, Jr.' heard of the plight of the Cuban Revolutionary Council, still confined by armed guards in a desolate shack. As the news of impending defeat finally reached the nominal leaders of the invasion, they clamored to be allowed to rejoin their own people. A call went to Washington, Schlesinger went to the President, who agreed that both Schlesinger and Berle ought to fly to Opa-Locka that night and confer with the Council.

By cruel circumstances, Tuesday evening the President had to put on white tie, tails and a smiling face for the traditional White House reception at which Congressmen are formally presented to Cabinet members. Nearly 450 persons were at the festive affair, and at 10:15 the President and his lady descended the main stairs into the entrance hall. Mrs. Kennedy wore a sleeveless, floor-length pink and white sheath, and a diamond clip bobbed in her bouffant hairdo. At a signal, the Marine Band struck up *Mr. Wonderful* and the President and First Lady whirled around the floor, smiling graciously at the applauding guests.

This was the incongruous setting when the President was informed that Richard M. Bissell wished to see him. Kennedy asked the CIA official to come to the White House, and others were summoned to join him. Secretary of State Rusk was called from a formal dinner for the Greek Premier, and he came to the President's White House office with Secretary of Defense McNamara, General Lemnitzer and Admiral Burke. An intense discussion lasted until the early morning hours. Bissell made an appeal for the use of United States airpower to help the otherwise doomed invaders. Admiral Burke concurred. But Secretary Rusk vigorously dissented, pointing out that the President himself had pledged that there would be no direct U.S. intervention. The President, whose confidence in his military and intelligence chiefs had been shaken and who was keenly aware of his own explicit pledge, could not be persuaded to plunge further down an uncertain path.

After hearing the arguments, the President turned down the appeal for a last-minute salvage operation. At this point, the "disposal problem" had come to its pathetic final disposition.

136

If Tuesday was harrowing for President Kennedy, it was calamitous for 1,500 or so men who were clinging like crabs to a tiny patch of Cuban shoreline. The day began, slightly after midnight, when a battery of 122 mm. howitzers began shelling the beachhead in support of militia units armed with Belgian and Czech submachine guns and Czech "four-mouth" rocket-throwers. Units of Soviet-built T-34 tanks, heavy artillery and anti-aircraft artillery, surrounded the beach perimeter. As Castro was to say later, "then, the attack was incessant, and we attacked them incessantly." Commanding the government forces was Captain (now major) Gullego Fernandez, a 6-foot regular army officer who was imprisoned by Batista.

The blackness of the tropical night concealed a bloody exchange. Castro's tanks rumbled up the perimeter of the rebel-held area, supported by the anti-aircraft guns firing at flat trajectory. Rebel tanks and artillery returned the fire; the swamps and beaches echoed with a roar of guns. Castro was massing his forces; from his headquarters at the Australia sugar mill, he deployed around the invaders a company of tanks, four batteries of 122 mm. howitzers, one battery of 37 mm. cannon, and a whole array of supporting units.

Inexorably, the superior force told. The Premier's troops forced the invaders to yield the village of Cayo Ramona, and as the rebels retreated another Castro batallion moved west to Playa Larga. By daybreak, his forces bolstered by additional tank and artillery companies, Castro was able to level an attack on Playa Girón itself, while other militia units divided the rebel army by cutting the columns retreating from Caya Ramona from the main force nearer the beach. By 10 a.m., the invaders were forced to fall back still further to protect the rear guard.

From all accounts, the outnumbered invaders fought bravely and well. They used their equipment intelligently and returned fire as best they could. Considering that the rebels had no command center, no air cover, no ambulances and no place to retreat to, they performed creditably and gallantly.

"If we only had more ammunition," an insurgent who was taken prisoner told one of the authors, "we could have held out—maybe even won." But the stores of ammunition went down with the *Houston*. Aloft, the rebel position was no better. Three more B-26's went down Tuesday and Castro had clear control of the air. At this point, the Premier claims in his account that F-86 Sabres appeared, but this does not square with other versions. It is possible that Castro was referring to Navy jets that were in the air over international waters.

By early afternoon, the press releases in Miami and New York had acquired a gloomier tone. Bulletin No. 4 issued by Lem Jones Associates at 1:20 p.m. stated:

> Peasants, workers and militia are joining the freedom front and aiding the rapidly expanding area already liberated by the Revolutionary Command.
>
> The Cuban Revolutionary Council announces that Cuban freedom fighters in the Matanzas area are being attacked by heavy Soviet tanks and MIG aircraft which have destroyed sizeable amounts of medical supplies and equipment.
>
> These humanitarian supplies were destined for the Cuban freedom fighters who are shedding their blood to overthrow the shackles of Communism.
>
> The Cuban Revolutionary Council is deeply grateful for the countless messages of support and encouragement pouring in from all parts of the world. Such demonstrations of international sympathy are convincing proof that freedom loving people of the world repudiate the Communistic slavery imposed by Castro over the Cuban people.

As Wednesday dawned, the perimeter held by the invaders had shrunk to the two beachheads of Playa Girón and Playa Larga. All during the night, the rebels had been shelled and a sense of defeat eroded morale. Behind Castro's lines, ambulances were careening to Havana with the wounded—but there were no ambulances for the battered invading forces.

In the air, insurgent B-26's made a vain attempt to bomb Castro's headquarters at the Australia sugar mill. Two more B-26's were downed, bringing the total lost by the invaders to ten. According to one version, jet fighters from the U.S.S. *Boxer* were supposed to have provided an air umbrella for one hour for the rebel bombers, but by mischance the B-26's came too early and the jets were still sitting on the carrier. This story, elaborated by Charles J. V. Murphy in his *Fortune* article, has not been officially confirmed. But Ulysses Carbo, one of the invaders, remarked to a reporter afterwards of that Wednesday morning: "I laid in the bushes and saw your airplanes, but it was too late." Assuredly, he was

138

right; the invasion had deteriorated to a point beyond rescue by a one-hour air monopoly for the invaders.

Meanwhile, in New York, Lem Jones Associates, Inc., issued Bulletin No. 5:

> In spite of continuous attacks by Soviet MIGs, heavy tanks and artillery forces the Revolutionary Command has completed the planned first phase of their military operation in the south of Cuba. This phase involved the successful establishment of contact with guerilla groups in the Escambray mountains.
>
> Numerous elements of the forces from the Cochinos Bay area have completed a movement north of Cienfuegos from which they will be able to reinforce the patriots already fighting in the mountains.
>
> It can also be revealed that additional guerrilla units have infiltrated central Matanzas Province. The heroic action of a small holding force which resisted Soviet tanks, artillery and aircraft during the last twenty hours, made possible this result.
>
> According to the Command's last information this force continues its valiant fight against tyranny.

By midmorning, Castro was moving in for the kill and had arrayed his forces along classical warfare lines, bearing down on the beaches with his 122 mm. howitzers, tanks and infantry. By 10 a.m., the Premier's troops had driven the rebels from the village of San Blas. The end was near in the afternoon; by 6 p.m., Castro's tanks began a relentless encircling thrust. Only one out of five rebel tanks was still in action. Slowly, the first invaders began surrendering as Castro's armor applied pressure. Some of the invaders eluded capture by fleeing in small boats and boarding a U.S. destroyer in international waters. Others tried to scramble through the swamps and somehow reach the Escambray mountains eighty miles away. It took five days for Castro finally to round up virtually all of the surviving invading army, some 1,200 troops in all. During the last waning hours, a radio ham in New Jersey heard a faint signal. "This is Cuba calling. Where will help come from? This is Cuba calling the free world. We need help in Cuba."

Playa Girón fell at 5:30 p.m. The news of the defeat was flashed from a walkie-talkie to the nearby U.S. destroyer. Castro himself exulted: "The invaders have been annihilated. The revolution has emerged victorious. It destroyed in less than 72 hours the army organized during many months by the imperialistic government of the United States."

The sad and needless tragedy ended not with a bang, but with a press release. At 9 p.m., this final communiqué was issued:

CUBAN REVOLUTIONARY COUNCIL
Via: Lem Jones Associates, Inc.
280 Madison Avenue
New York, New York
ORegon 9-5636
IMMEDIATE RELEASE
April 19 - 9 p.m.

Bulletin No. 6

The Revolutionary Council wishes to make a prompt and emphatic statement in the face of recent astonishing public announcement from uninformed sources.

The statement indicates that "several thousand" Cuban patriots have fallen in the battle which took place today in southern Cuba. This is a pronouncement which will certainly please Castro but would dishearten the Cuban people who are eagerly waiting to break the chains that bind them to Communism.

The recent landings in Cuba have been constantly though inaccurately described as an invasion. It was, in fact, a landing mainly of supplies and support for our patriots who have been fighting in Cuba for months and was numbered in the hundreds, not the thousands.

Regretfully, we admit tragic losses in today's action among a small holding force which courageously fought Soviet tanks and artillery while being attacked by Russian MIG aircraft—a gallantry which allowed the major portion of our landing party to reach the Escambray mountains.

We did not expect to topple Castro immediately or without setbacks. And it is certainly true that we did not expect to face, unscathed, Soviet armaments directed by Communist advisers. We did and survived!

The struggle for the freedom of six million Cubans continues!

So it happened. Viewed strictly as a military venture, everything that could possibly go wrong on the Bay of Pigs seemed to go wrong. It turned into a war without a battle, and encounter that was over almost before it began. The assumption was that the invaders could hold the Bay of Pigs long enough to fly in a provisional government—and then, if matters went badly, the provisional government could appeal to the outside world for help and the United States would be in a position to respond.

But, incredibly, little attention was given to the possibility that the invaders might never hold the beachhead. Calamity followed upon calamity to make this the melancholy outcome. First, there was the failure to assure control of the air. Second, there was the inability of the paratroop detachments to blow up the causeways and paved roads leading into the beachhead area, a failure that has still not been fully explained. Third, there was the disaster of the sinking of the *Houston*—and with it, the vital communications system and the ammunition stores.

In effect, what happened was that some 1,500 men were dumped on a beach without cover from the sky or from artillery aboard ships at sea. There was no real command center and no provision for alternative plans in the event of a major disaster. The men on the beach behaved well under catastrophically demoralizing circumstances—remember that the invaders had been solemnly assured air cover. The insurgents fired as best they could at Castro's encircling force—but Fidel had only to wait until their ammunition ran out before mopping up with scarcely a fight. This is precisely what occurred in the invasion that never had a chance to succeed.

VIII

In Washington, Wednesday was the morning after for President Kennedy, and during the darkest moment of his first year, the young Chief Executive was impressively composed. The day was occupied by lengthy meetings at which the President set the tone by refusing to vent his anger in recriminations. Mr. Kennedy and Harry Truman, so unalike in background and temperament, shared the inner iron that enables a leader to assume final responsibility without flinching or heaping blame on subordinates.

In the Cabinet room, congressional leaders as well as members of his official family were gathered to discuss the debacle. Mr. Kennedy, who calmly smoked two cigars, made no attempt to sugar over the news. Nor did Senator Richard Russell and Representative Carl Vinson, chairmen of the armed services committees of Congress, conceal their feeling that the United States had suffered a cruel defeat.

After the meeting, the President told his aide, Theodore Sorensen, to scrap a speech that had been prepared for a meeting the next day of the American Society of Newspaper Editors. The talk would have to be about Cuba.

The six leaders of the Cuban Revolutionary Council, in the meantime, had been flown to the Capital in an Air Force plane from their enforced confinement at Opa-Locka. The President agreed to see them. Dr. Miró Cardona, president of the Council, spoke for the Cubans and made two requests. First, he asked that the United States intervene directly to salvage Operation Pluto. The President explained that this could not be done in the light of his repeated pledges against direct intervention. Secondly, the Cuban appealed to the President to do all that he could to save the lives of the captured rebels. Dr. Miró Cardona's son was one of the prisoners, and the President responded to the father's moving appeal by promising that he would do all that was in his power to save the men. This promise was the genesis of the President's subsequent decision to take up Premier Castro's impulsive offer to swap the prisoners for tractors. Throughout the meeting, the Cubans bore the defeat with dignity. The President was apologetic about their confinement and assured the Cubans that they were free to go where they wished.

On Thursday, the President met the press, rounding out a curious cycle. Almost exactly two years after Castro spoke before the ASNE, the President of the United States was addressing the same audience from the same rostrum—the flower-decked head table in the Statler-Hilton's main ballroom. The editors and their wives rose from their seats and gave Mr. Kennedy prolonged applause as the strains of *Hail to the Chief* heralded his entrance.

The President's composure once more was impressive, but the strain told. His speech was not an immortal utterance. He abjured contrition and took an aggressive tack that was bound to inspire the expectation of something dramatic to come which would erase the humiliating defeat. The rhetoric was Churchillian, but the tone was of a thwarted leader finding release from a sense of defeat through a rush of martial words:

If the nations of this hemisphere should fail to meet their commitments against outside Communist penetration, then this government will not hesitate in meeting its primary obligations, which are the security of this nation. Should that time ever come, we do not intend to be lectured on intervention by those whose charac-

142

ter was stamped for all time on the bloody streets of Budapest.

The message of Cuba, of Laos, of Latin America, these messages are all the same. The complacent, the self-indulgent, the soft societies are about to be swept away with the debris of history. Only the strong, only the industrious, only the determined, only the courageous, only the visionary, who determine the real nature of our struggle can possibly survive.

I am determined upon our system's survival and success, regardless of the cost, and regardless of the peril.

After this flourish of trumpets, the news of the following days was bound to be anticlimactic. Nothing happened to Castro, and Mr. Kennedy's primary follow-up was a round of meetings that came to include General Eisenhower, General Douglas MacArthur, Richard M. Nixon, Governor Nelson Rockefeller and Senator Barry M. Goldwater. Within the Administration, the President assigned his brother, Attorney General Robert Kennedy, and General Maxwell Taylor, to examine the procedures that led to the debacle. The results of the inquiry are still secret.

In public, the President continued his policy of avoiding reproaches. "There is an old saying," he remarked ruefully at his April 21 news conference, "that victory has a hundred fathers and defeat is an orphan." Considering the scale of the disaster, it is striking that there were no firings and no major resignations. Indeed, the only public chiding administered by the President was aimed at the press. Administration circles were clearly vexed with the press, contending that too much publicity stripped the "cover" from the invasion. Some officials even seemed to imply that the invasion failed because of excessive publicity. On April 27, Mr. Kennedy spoke before the American Newspaper Publishers Association in New York, and at one point admonished:

> Every newspaper now asks itself, with respect to every story: "Is it news?" All I suggest is that you add the question: "Is it in the national interest?" .... And should the press of America consider and recommend the voluntary assumption of specific steps or machinery, I can assure that we will cooperate wholeheartedly with those recommendations.

To many editors and reporters, keenly sensitive to the

143

difficulties of covering the "black" service, the President's apparent call for self-censorship was perplexing. In the specific instance of the Cuban invasion, the operation was scarcely a "secret" to Fidel Castro. The very scale of the operation, the laxness of security, the volubility of Cuban exiles, the crude hoax of the pre-invasion raid—all these assured that Castro himself would not be "fooled." It was not the press that embarrassed the Government. The Government embarrassed itself by sponsoring a venture that sought to put a free press in the position of conveying flimsy lies that might more appropriately appear in *Pravda* or *Revolución*.

IX

In Cuba, it was a mad carnival in which a gifted ringmaster missed not a single showman's trick. For five successive nights, Fidel Castro gloatingly paraded his prisoners before TV cameras. Viewers in Key West could watch the audience chant "to the wall" as an announcer asked Cubans to telephone if they spotted any "war criminals" among the captives.

A woman burst forward and identified Ramón Calviño as a Batista torturer; even exiles acknowledged that this "freedom fighter" had fifteen murders on his record. Others among the prisoners were broken and confused. Some talked back spunkily, including Carlos Varona, son of "Tony" Varona, who snapped back: "If you have so many people on your side, why don't you hold elections?"

May Day was boisterous in Havana, and Premier Castro made it official by proclaiming his country a "socialist" state. Soon, he began playing cat-and-mouse with the United States by putting up his prisoners for barter and then haggling over how many tractors each man was worth. The negotiations came to nothing, but not before a flock of newspapermen entered Cuba and were given a grand battlefield tour by the Premier, who was every bit the great general musing philosophically about battles past.

Castro's battlefield tour provides perhaps the best epilogue to the Cuban invasion. One of the authors vividly recalls the "Maximum Leader's" at Playa Girón on June 15, 1961, putting his foot on the wreckage of a rebel B-26 and asking his guests to come closer.

"You see," he said, briskly waving his cigar, "they underestimated us and they used their own forces incorrectly."

Around him as he talked was the semi-finished workers' beach resort at the edge of the marshes.

The Premier listed as the elements of his victory his control of the air as well as tactical errors in the deployment and timing of the attacking force. During his trek around the beach Castro said that he had no idea where the landing would come and that he expected his enemies to make several simultaneous landings instead of committing all their forces on a single front.

"That was their first error," he expounded. "And because they had established a large beachhead, it became an urgent political problem for us to oust them as quickly as possible so that they would not establish a government here."

Castro said that his government kept most of its heavy military equipment in Havana, and as soon as news of the attack had come, flat-bed trucks were ordered to start carrying tanks to the area. That the attackers permitted this to happen, he said, was their second major error. The paratroopers, he held, were brought on the scene too late to cut communications.

Then, he went on, several units of the rebel army waited too long after the first wave went ashore thus allowing Cuban aircraft to sink the ship *Houston* with its batallion of troops and communications equipment. The ship, her superstructure jutting from the water, could be seen from the beach where we talked.

Continuing his critique, the Premier elaborated his belief that the rebels had used their paratroopers "too conservatively." When asked how they should have been used, he wagged his finger and laughed, saying, "I am not going to tell you that."

The problem, he said, is that the rebels did not have a "guerrilla mentality, like we do, and they acted like a conventional army." He was wearing his usual olive-green fatigue boots and brown beret during a lecture he obviously enjoyed. "We used guerrilla tactics to infiltrate their lines, while attacking steadily from the air and on the ground," he said. "You must never let the enemy sleep."

He was in agreement with the surviving rebels that they had first-rate equipment and excellent fire-power. Most of the equipment was captured intact, including four tanks in serviceable condition. Castro conceded that his forces had made the error of advancing on the open road that rises above the quicksand of the marshes where they were easy targets for rebel mortars and aircraft.

The Premier would not say how many men he had in

action, but he said that his losses neared ninety men—most killed by aircraft action. The rebel survivors said they were sure they had killed many more.

Throughout, the Cuban stressed the role of his airpower and said that the invaders had made a major miscalculation in believing that their April 15 raid had destroyed aircraft on the ground. Actually, he said, no aircraft had been destroyed because they had been dispersed. When the invasion came, he continued, he had more planes than pilots to fly them. Ground crews worked feverishly to put as many aircraft into flying shape as possible.

Visiting the beachhead two months later, it was difficult to imagine that heavy fighting had taken place there. There was a crater caused by a 500-pound bomb near a beach house. On a concrete landing strip that the rebels held briefly there was the wreckage of a B-26. Nearby lay a rocket with United States Navy markings.

And the sky above was as blue as the Caribbean, as deceptively peaceful as the waves lapping against the shore.

CHAPTER EIGHT

▷ **EPILOGUE**

Looking backward through the telescope of retrospect a year later, the Cuban invasion seems a less implausible catastrophe than it did in the cruel April of 1961. Time, however, has not scaled down the dimension of the fiasco. The Cuban invasion was, as Theodore Draper has remarked, one of those rare events in history—a perfect failure.

It was a failure of mind, of imagination, of common sense—a failure that seems all the more grotesque now as the bright insiders in the Kennedy Administration discuss it with a certain mordant relish. It solved nothing. It won nothing—indeed, perhaps its one redeeming virtue was that it was settled with blessed speed before thousands of brave men rounded up in Cuban jails were slaughtered by a panicky regime.

As a mechanical failure, defeat was built in by the very flimsy pretense on which the invasion was based. For political reasons, and surely not unreasonable ones, President

Kennedy felt that overt involvement by the United States was out of the question. Mr. Kennedy did not want what his aides described as a "Hungary in reverse" in which it would seem to the world that Washngton was no different from Moscow and would act just as ruthlessly to crush a rebellious neighbor.

From beginning to end, therefore, the pretense was officially maintained that the invaders had the hearty good wishes of the United States, but little else. The seemingly obvious fact that it would be impossible to conceal American complicity—at least in a free society with a free press able to hear the gossip of loquacious Cubans—this fact never seemed to dawn on the operators at the top.

Mr. Kennedy set the ground rules by proscribing any direct United States support. Both the CIA and the Joint Chiefs of Staff, let it be stressed again, accepted this limitation—and acquiesced in every modification aimed at preserving the fiction of a "spontaneous" Cuban invasion. Yet these modifications had the effect of perhaps fatally impairing the military feasibility of an already risky plan.

The key to the military outcome, in terms of holding a beachhead, was largely control of the air. In order to conceal the United States role, it was agreed that no American pilots would participate, that no planes would fly from either mainland United States or Puerto Rico, and that only obsolete prop-driven planes would be supplied to the invaders. Finally, at the last minute, a second air strike aimed at crippling Castro's air power was canceled. The net effect of these self-imposed restraints was to enable Castro to sink a good part of the invasion armada before the fight had really begun. In the air battles over the Bay of Pigs, the lumbering rebel B-26's had no protection against the faster Castro T-33 trainer jets and Sea Furies. Yet within the limitations of operation, it was impossible to supply the invaders with fighters because the base in Guatemala was beyond fighter range.

As a military failure, the debacle might have been prevented *if* the Joint Chiefs had frankly advised that the self-imposed limitations robbed the venture of a chance to succeed. The Joint Chiefs approved the plan, apparently without looking ahead to the next moves in the chess game based on Castro's capabilities. They did not insist on contingency plans based on the possibility of partial or total failure.

Mechanical failure was also built in by the very assignment to the CIA of a military-political task beyond its competence. With no independent checks operating on the

147

CIA, the Agency quickly became the captive rather than the master of its own operation. Lulled by its easy earlier success in Guatemala, the CIA over-estimated its ability to manipulate history. Step by step, the Agency became infatuated with its own judgment as it plunged deeper into a labyrinth of its own making. Instead of a hard-headed, realistic plan, the Agency opted to gamble.

In February 1960, President Eisenhower gave the Agency authorization to proceed with the training of an exile force. By early fall, the camps in Guatemala were in full swing and an army of about 500 was in existence. At this point, the CIA thought in terms of a multiple operation involving a series of scattered landings tied in with an underground insurrection. But the Agency had little patience with or knowledge of the Cuban underground, and as time went on more and more reliance was placed on a single, all-or-nothing invasion strike. Indeed the steady expansion of the exile army had the effect of predetermining the way it would be used.

The CIA's misadventures in political policies tied in closely with its military preconceptions. Distrusting the underground, wary of the left-liberal MRP, CIA agents placed their main reliance on aging Cuban politicians of honorable intentions but limited appeal and on an adventurous youngster with conservative leanings who was cast in the role of Guatemala's Castillo Armas. If the invasion had succeeded, the government literally glued together by the CIA would have seemed to all the world like pliant proxies for Washington, in the pattern of Colonel Castillo Armas in Guatemala.

Taken together, the CIA operation was like a car decked out with flashy accessories—a musical horn, a two-way radio and tailfins three feet high—but lacking a motor. The motor could not be installed by outside mechanics—the vital missing part was the participation of the Cuban people in whose name the invasion was fought. From the beginning, there was a preconception that Cubans so loathed Fidel Castro that they would jump to the barricades at the first opportunity and throw the rascal out. But there was more to the Castro revolution than a simple question of communism. Although many of the Cubans in Miami lost because of Castro, hundreds of thousands of Cubans on the island gained. A meaningful insurrection would have to come from within, and the incentive for revolt would have to be stronger than diatribes, no doubt deserved, about a Red specter that meant little to *guajiros* in the hills. Even if American air power had enabled the rebels to hang on a

148

while longer on the beach, it is highly debatable whether there would have been any mass defections from Castro. External invasion was the form of attack that would best enable Castro to rally even wavering supporters. And the fact that the CIA failed to alert the underground neutralized the one internal group that might have altered the outcome.

Thus, the invasion accomplished just the reverse of its objectives. Instead of eliminating Castro, it strengthened his hold on his people and inflated his prestige in the world. Instead of isolating Castroism, it ended up by momentarily isolating the United States. And in place of dramatizing the aggressive intent of Castroite communism, it seemed to dramatize the bullying tactics of the United States.

II

It was a failure of mechanics and imagination—and it was also a moral failure. The immorality, in our view, did not lie in assisting the genuine democrats who opposed the perversion of the Cuban revolution. Rather, it lay in the way the assistance was rendered, leaving this country with only a few shreds of defense against the charge of violating national, hemisphere and international laws. Yet, in fact, the United States was not willing to go the limit, so that America earned the opprobrium for transgressing without winning any of the benefits.

Some feel that the United States should hew to the strictest letter of nonintervention pledges, withholding either overt or covert help for democrats who are struggling against some odious foreign despot. But adherants of this view must contend with an argument made more than a century ago by John Stuart Mill, the unimpeachable apostle of liberal political philosophy. In his little-known essay, "A Few Words on Non-Intervention," first published in 1859, Mill wrote:

> The doctrine of non-intervention, to be a legitimate principle of morality, must be accepted by all governments. The despot must consent to be bound by it as well as the free states. Unless they do, the profession comes to this miserable issue—that the wrong side may help the wrong, but the right must not help the right.
>
> Intervention to enforce non-intervention is always rightful, always moral, if not always prudent. . . . It might not have been right for England (even apart

from the question of prudence) to have taken part with Hungary in its noble struggle against Austria, although the Austrian government in Hungary was in some sense a foreign yoke.

But when, the Hungarians having shown themselves likely to prevail in this struggle, the Russian despot intervened, and joining his forces to that of Austria, delivered back the Hungarians, bound hand and foot, to their exasperated oppressors. It would have been an honorable and virtuous act on the part of England to have declared that this should not be; and that if the Russians gave assistance to the wrong side, England would aid the right.

A great deal has changed in the world since 1859, although the Russian despot still binds Hungary hand and foot. In the military sphere, nuclear weapons have given more importance to the question of the prudence of intervention. In world diplomacy, treaties now set some limits on overt intervention.

But in Cuba, would it have been more "moral" if the Russians gave assistance to the wrong side while the United States turned its back on the right? The Cuban people have by now become the victims of what Mill called a "native tyranny upheld by foreign arms." Surely it is dissembling to invoke the phrase "self-determination" in discussing the plight of a people who since Castro took power have never had a chance to cast a vote, despite the most explicit promises that elections would be held. When Raúl Roa sanctimoniously lectures the United States on nonintervention, it is well to remember that his own government refuses to respect the same principle.

We have attempted in our narrative to point out that United States blunders abetted Castro's communization of Cuba. But we cannot accept the argument that the United States "drove" Castro into Khrushchev's arms. Getting the "Maximum Leader" to embrace the Russians was like bribing Don Juan to have a date with Venus.

In the light of the foreign-backed autocracy that Castro has imposed on Cuba, in our view there was nothing immoral about helping the dictator's opponents. But surely prudence should have indicated a quite different method of aid. The United States is party to a series of treaties that proscribe overt intervention into a neighbor's affairs. These were the same treaties cited repeatedly by the State Department in condemning Castro's own attempts to "export" his revolution.

Moreover, in Latin America, the United States has yet to live down the long era when a squadron of Marines and gunboat were regarded as the indispensable tools of Caribbean diplomacy. Latin Americans are hypersensitive to the question of intervention, and the invasion was an affront to those sensibilities. Remember that in April 1961, Castro was also an unsullied idol to millions of Latin Americans, who saw events in Cuba from a quite different perspective than they were seen in Washington.

For all these reasons, the United States approach to helping the forces of freedom in Cuba ought to have taken a different and more sophisticated form. In the long run, no communist satellite can flourish only 90 miles from the soil of Florida. Not even the euphoria of revolution could forever blind the Cuban people to the simple reality that their island has no future in trading its major crop halfway around the world to a country that has ample sugar stocks of its own. Finally, few people in the world have shown a more persistent willingness to rise up again and again to oppose odious tyrants. Indeed, Mr. Khrushchev, with a peasant's shrewd sense, was smarter in this respect than the CIA. While Moscow has found it useful to provide help for Castro, the Russians have refused to invest their rubles heavily in a country with so uncertain a future and such effervescent leadership.

The invasion was an attempt to hurry history; a slower, surer, more politically defensible course would have been to provide discreet help to the Cuban underground. Such assistance could have been genuinely covert, and even if detected, could have been disclaimed officially by the United States. Castro himself, it should be recalled, smuggled guns from Florida.

Intelligence sources maintain that the underground was not sufficiently "security" conscious, that the Castro police was too efficient, and that it was difficult to smuggle "communicators" with radio equipment into Cuba. Strangely, the CIA was able to overcome the logistic problems of organizing an entire miniature army in Guatemala, but was seemingly unable to manage sneaking a few men, radios and explosives into an island 90 miles from Florida.

In any event, this course was not followed before (or after) the invasion. Three times, within the space of a decade, the United States has managed to undercut its best democratic friends in Cuba. The first time was during the

151

Batista era, when Washington paid little attention to the embattled, and noncommunist, opposition groups; the second time was after the Castro revolution, when clumsy United States policy seemed time and again to play into Castro's hands and to impair the influence of moderates; finally, there was the invasion, in which the United States engendered a sense of betrayal among Cuban democrats in exile and in the underground.

It is not a happy record.

III

Who, in the end, was responsible for the Cuban calamity? It is difficult to single out villains, because the tragedy sprang from a conspiracy of circumstance. Clearly, the President of the United States must accept the responsibility for approving the venture and for failing to heed the counsel of his own common sense. And whatever the reason, the President's decision to cancel the second aid strike before the invasion was a serious blow to an already risky plan—although those who talk only about this decision often conveniently overlook the other mistakes for which the President bore more limited responsibility.

The men around Mr. Kennedy, too, must share in the blame. These bright and able aides failed to see that the scale of the invasion was too big to conceal United States complicity. Strangely, no effort was made to probe deeper into the Miami operation despite the warnings that American prestige was hinging on the work of men miscast for their role. And the Joint Chiefs, as we have pointed out, also failed to apply the brakes by using some foresight about the capability of an adversary.

In essence, the invasion was rooted in a military miscalculation compounded by political miscalculations that in turn rested on intelligence miscalculations. The burden of the institutional blame falls most heavily on the Agency that conceived and directed the invasion itself. The CIA was simply not equipped to make the military and political decisions thrust upon it. The Agency, in building up the invasion force, became involved in questions of almost metaphysical nicety in trying to conceal its own hand. Obsolete bombers were permitted the invaders—presumably because they could be purchased on the open market—but obsolete aircraft carriers that might have assured air support were witheld because that might give the show away.

In the command strategy, CIA operatives seemed to pass

over the points of psychological preparation that are as vital as military preparation. The island itself was not thrown into confusion by preparatory sabotage; and the invaders themselves landed on the beach with the complete confidence that air support would shelter them. Thus the island was not prepared for the invasion—and the invaders were not prepared for the devastating blow to morale that came when Castro's planes dominated the air.

Yet the CIA was not behaving idiotically; it was in many senses responding to the insulated rationalism that infects a sheltered bureaucracy. Indeed, if there is an institutional villain, it is bureaucracy itself—that hulking, stubborn giant that seemingly can only look where it has been and not whither is is tending.

Max Weber, the German sociologist and great natural historian of bureaucracy, would not have been overly surprised by the Cuban invasion. Glance at these attributes that Weber detected in the modern bureaucracy (quoted from H. H. Gerth and C. Wright Mills, translators of *From Max Weber: Essays in Sociology):*

> Under normal conditions, the power position of a fully developed bureaucracy is always overtowering. The "political master finds himself in the position of the "dilettante" who stands opposite the "expert," facing the trained official who stands within the management of administration.

> Every bureaucracy seeks to increase the superiority of the professionally informed by keeping their knowledge and intentions secret. Bureaucratic administration always tends to be an administration of "secret sessions": in so far as it can, it hides its knowledge and actions from criticism.

> The concept of the "official secret" is the specific invention of bureaucracy, and nothing is so fanatically defended by the bureaucracy as this attitude. . . . In facing a parliament, the bureaucracy, out of a sure power instinct, fights every attempt of parliament to gain knowledge by means of its own experts or from interest groups.

> The absolute monarch is powerless opposite the superior knowledge of the bureaucratic expert—in a certain sense more powerless than any other political head. All the scornful decrees of Frederick the Great concerning the "abolition of serfdom" were derailed, as it were, in the official mechanism simply ignored them as the occasional ideas of a dilettante.

Max Weber was propounding the traits of bureaucracy in general; the case of a secret bureaucracy raises special questions even more difficult to answer because the bureaucrat is free from the normal controls of parliamentary inquiry or press comment. Once it has ventured down a blind alley, there is little built into our system that can redirect the secret bureaucracy on a different course.

In the case of the Cuban invasion, a segment of a powerful bureaucracy committed itself to a specific approach to a particular problem. Its money, its prestige, its *esprit de corps* were enrolled in a project the bureaucratic experts adjudged to be sound. The wheels ground forward and the momentum of the bureaucracy seemed to become irreversible as it swept along an entire government behind a plan that rested on the secret knowledge of those who were steering in darkness. One overall lesson of the Cuban invasion is that in the cathedral of bureaucracy an outspoken atheist can perform an essential function.

IV

But there are further "sobering lessons for us all to learn," as the President said on April 20, 1961, when the gall of defeat was bitterest. Surely a few general reflections on the role of the CIA are in order. Palpably, the agency is in a difficult position. Its officers cannot—or at least should not—engage in public debate in defending the CIA's deeds. Obvious blunders receive sensational headlines; quiet successes go (as they should) unreported. At the higher levels, the Agency is staffed by men of probity and experience, and one can assume that the CIA does a competent job in gathering information.

Yet during the past years, the Agency has tended to assume an activist role in many areas of the world—a tendency that was especially marked during the Eisenhower years when a passive Chief Executive allowed the CIA wide lattitude. The result of the near-autonomous status was not always happy. American ambassadors complained that at times the CIA seemed to be running its own foreign policy in the field; reporters exchanged horror stories about what CIA operatives were doing in scattered corners of the world, notably in Southeast Asia. A recurring theme was the tendency of CIA agents, often working with military mission officers, to gravitate to the right and support the most effusive but often least effective anti-communists.

Some of this bias may spring from a selection process that frequently brings into the Agency covert operators whose

154

patriotic zeal does more credit to their hearts than heads. To this can be added the inherited legacy of the CIA from its predecessor agency, the Office of Strategic Services. When World War II was over, most of the abler veterans of the OSS returned to civilian work. But those who found a vocation in the conspirational twilight world of the "black" service tended to stay on, and many later joined the CIA.

The conspiratorial personality at its worst is memorably described by Rebecca West in *The Meaning of Treason:*

> Sweet it is to be not what the next man thinks one, but far more powerful . . . to charm the confidences from the unsuspecting stranger; to put one's finger through the whimsical darkness and touch the fabric of state . . . and to do all this for nobility's sake.
>
> It is the misfortune of our age . . . that the life of the political conspirator offers the man of restricted capacity but imaginative energy greater excitement and satisfaction than he can ever derive from overt activities.

The description snugly fits the bizarre cast that romped around Miami, making and breaking future governments of Cuba. At one point, reportedly, Captain Artime jokingly offered the job of Cuban Sports Commissioner to Mr. Bender who, with equal hilarity, accepted. "They come by plane, by train and by bus," one exile in Miami observed, "and in half an hour everyone knows who they are." Indeed, Mr. Bender's telephone number was casually offered to a reporter in a bar by a Cuban friend within an hour of the newspaperman's arrival in Miami in March 1961.

Power corrupts; secret power intoxicates. Our men in Miami lived beyond the law's reach, spent vast and unaccounted-for funds; posted satisfying cryptic reports to Washington; and savored to the hilt the giddying sense of being the secret makers of history.

This is not a cast of characters to whom one would confidently entrust the most delicate mission of making foreign policy in a controversy close to home but with ramifications around the world. Here, ultimately, rests one of the mainsprings of the Cuban tragedy: the delegation of American prestige into the hands of agents who by normal personnel standards might be adjudged misfits or adventurers.

One painful lesson of the Cuban invasion is that there must be limits to the kind of clandestine ventures that the CIA may sponsor. Put succinctly, the Agency should be an instrument and not an originator of foreign policy, and the scale of its operations ought not to compromise the free institutions the CIA is defending. It is one thing to tailor covert operations to fit within the framework of a free society, and quite another to try and remake the free society to suit the convenience of a secret bureaucracy. In organizing a miniature army recruited from American soil, the CIA was counting on a degree of collaboration for essentially lawless activities that only a monolithic despotism can exact. That it was done so badly suggests that this kind of clandestine operation is not one that Americans can do well. That so many political blunders were made suggests that the founding fathers were wise to delegate the administration of foreign affairs to the Department of State.

A larger lesson involves the total American reaction to the Cuban revolution. The invasion plan was in some sense a logical extension of prevailing attitudes to a revolutionary situation. Like it or not, Americans must learn to work within the swift currents of change that are sweeping through the world. In terms of simple realism, it is impossible to emulate King Canute and order the waves to recede.

If the CIA plan, based on its Guatemala success, was not an attempt to reverse the wave,—it was clearly carried out in a fashion that implied the tide did not exist. Like so much of the American reaction to the Cuban revolution, the CIA did not take seriously enough the depth and breadth of the change signified by the emergence of Fidel Castro. There was a reluctance to face the fact that Cuba was in rebellion against the past—a past in which American interests were deeply implicated. What happened in Cuba, in its initial phases, was a declaration of independence; if subsequently Castro perverted the revolution, he has not stifled the demand for independence. Indeed, the same impulse that he once encouraged may yet turn against him and bring about his downfall. The Cuban drama has not yet ended, and the island's genuine partisans of freedom will surely still have the last word.

ACKNOWLEDGMENTS

For obvious reasons, the authors cannot list the names of the many Cubans and Americans whose confidential interviews went into the making of this chronicle. What can be said is that we have made an honest effort to seek out varying views and to subject points in dispute to careful examination. But in describing an event of such manifest complexity, some errors may be inescapable.

As journalists, the authors have followed the Cuban revolution since its first days and know most of the leaders whose decisions played a part in the story. Besides our first-hand experience, we have drawn on the vast body of published material about Cuba and the April invasion.

Among the post-mortems, Stewart Alsop's "The Lessons of the Cuban Disaster," *Saturday Evening Post*, June 24, 1961; Theodore Draper, "Cuba and U. S. Policy," *New Leader*, June 5, 1961; and Charles J. V. Murphy, "Cuba: The Record Set Straight," *Fortune*, September, 1961; are especially useful, although the Murphy material must be consulted with caution since the writer's facts and interpretation are in serious dispute.

Other articles worth examining include Stuart Novins, "The Invasion That Could Not Succeed," *Reporter*, May 11, 1961; Louis J. Halle, "Lessons of the Cuban Blunder," *New Republic*, June 5, 1961; and the reports of the two major news magazines, "The Cuban Disaster," *Time*, April 28, 1961; and "Cuba: What Went Wrong?" *Newsweek*, May 1, 1961. The May 6, 1961 "Letter from Washington" by Richard Rovere in the *New Yorker* contains valuable sidelights. Michael Walzer, "Cuba: The Invasion and the Consequences," *Dissent*, June, 1961, is a view from the left. See also Ronald Hilton, "The Cuba Trap," *Nation*, May 7, 1961. Hanson W. Baldwin presented a military interpretation in a two-part series in the New York *Times* beginning July 31, 1961. "The Exiles' Story," a four-part series by George Sherman, appeared in the Washington *Star* commencing on May 17, 1961. "What Went Wrong?" a critique in the May 1, 1961 *New Republic*, presents an informed analysis.

The problem of the press is discussed in Douglass Cater and Charles Bartlett, "Is All the News Fit to Print?" *Reporter*, May 11, 1961; and in a master's thesis, *The Cuban Invasion and the American Press*, now being submitted to George Washington University by Allen Bradford. In the mass of official literature, the most memorable State Department White Paper is entitled *Cuba*, Department of State Publication 7171, Released April 1961. The transcript of post-mortem hearings conducted by a Senate Foreign Relations Subcommittee has not yet been made public.

On the Cuban side, we have drawn on *Playa Giron*, an 114-page booklet published in Havana and giving the Castro version of the fight. Ernesto Guevara's *Guerrilla Warfare* is now available in translation, published by Frederick Praeger, New York, 1961.

We also owe special thanks to the many busy persons who generously gave us their time in order that this second draft of history might not be needlessly in error. It goes without saying, however, that any errors of fact or judgment rest solely with the authors, and that our opinions are not to be attributed to any person or institution other than ourselves.

INDEX

160